Literature,
Language,
and
Politics

Literature, Language, and Politics

Edited by
Betty Jean Craige

The University of Georgia Press
Athens and London

© 1988 by the University of Georgia Press
Athens, Georgia 30602.
The contributors to this volume retain copyright to their individual essays.
All rights reserved

Set in Times Roman with Helvetica display.

The paper in this book meets the guidelines for permanence and durability of the Committee on Production Guidelines for Book Longevity of the Council on Library Resources.

Printed in the United States of America

92 91 90 89 88   5 4 3 2 1

Library of Congress Cataloging in Publication Data

Literature, language, and politics / edited by Betty Jean Craige.
    p.   cm.
    Includes papers presented at a forum sponsored by the MLA Commission on the Status of Women in the Profession, in December 1987.
    Includes bibliographies.
    Contents: The two criticisms / by Paul Lauter—On the rhetoric of racism in the profession / by Henry Louis Gates, Jr.—Dancing between right and left / by Annette Kolodny—Language politics in the USA / by Ana Celia Zentella—The right moves / by Ellen Messer-Davidow—Politics and academic research / by Catharine R. Stimpson—An alternative to educational fundamentalism / by Gerald Graff.
    ISBN 0-8203-1109-X (alk. paper).
    ISBN 0-8203-1110-3 (pbk.: alk. paper)
    1. Politics and literature—United States.
2. Literature—Philosophy. 3. Literature, Modern—20th century—History and criticism.
4. United States—Politics and government—1981– 5. Education, Higher—Social aspects—United States. I. Craige, Betty Jean. II. Modern Language Association. Commission on the Status of Women in the Profession.
PN51.L5743 1988
810'.9'0054—dc19   88-20801
                                          CIP

British Library Cataloging in Publication Data available

Contents

Preface   vii

Acknowledgments   ix

1 The Two Criticisms: Structure, Lingo, and Power in the
Discourse of Academic Humanists, by Paul Lauter   1

2 On the Rhetoric of Racism in the Profession,
by Henry Louis Gates, Jr.   20

3 Dancing Between Left and Right: Feminism and the Academic
Minefield in the 1980s, by Annette Kolodny   27

4 Language Politics in the U.S.A.: The English-Only Movement,
by Ana Celia Zentella   39

5 The Right Moves: Conservatism and Higher Education, by
Ellen Messer-Davidow   54

6 Politics and Academic Research, by Catharine R. Stimpson   84

7 Teach the Conflicts: An Alternative to Educational
Fundamentalism, by Gerald Graff   99

List of Contributors   110

Preface   Betty Jean Craige

The 1980s have witnessed in government, religion, and education the rise of what is being called the New Right, apparently a backlash against the perceived liberalism of the 1960s. Religious fundamentalists, recognizing (like their left-wing adversaries) that texts impart values, are attempting to control the curriculum of public grade schools. "Educational fundamentalists," as Gerald Graff calls those who "blame the crisis of higher education and the humanities on a loss of consensus about fundamental purposes," have won support from the general public through such best-sellers as Allan Bloom's *The Closing of the American Mind* and E. D. Hirsch's *Cultural Literacy;* they seek to institute a common core curriculum, which former Secretary of Education William Bennett says must consist of the texts that epitomize "the civilization of the West." Another group striving to establish a culturally homogeneous America, the advocates of "English-only" legislation, have in thirteen states passed laws that declare English the official language of the nation. What these various movements have in common is fear of cultural "fragmentation."

Critics argue that the nostalgia for "traditional values," which has characterized the Reagan presidency, is a dangerous yearning for a time that never was, an imaginary epoch in our country's history when supposedly all were adherents to the same religious creed, all were English-speakers, all readers and cherishers of the "classics." These critics question the motives of the educational fundamentalists for making portions of the Western canon the center of the college curriculum, the proposed methods for achieving a consensus on what should be taught, and the possible consequences of the efforts to do so. Who decides, these critics ask, what texts constitute the "civilization of the West"? What values does such a core curriculum impart to our society? What texts does it exclude?

Obviously the success of the New Right in arousing public interest in a traditional liberal arts education and in English-only laws affects profoundly the work of scholars and teachers of literature and language in this country. That success is prompting, however, a thorough investigation of the conservatives' program and of the values they wish to "reinstate," as well as an exploration of disciplinary practices. Henry Louis Gates, Jr., Gerald Graff, Annette Kolodny, Paul Lauter, Ellen Messer-Davidow, Catharine Stimpson, and Ana Celia Zentella, who have contributed the essays published for the first time in this volume, are among the prominent thinkers seeking to expose and explain the sometimes hidden ideological purposes of the New Right agenda. The reason for publishing *Literature, Language, and Politics* is to show that such apparently distinct phenomena as English-only legislation, the rise of religious fundamentalism, and the back-to-basics movement belong to the same ideological model, a fact that participants in the discipline of literature and language study must understand if education is to remain truly liberal.

Acknowledgments

The origin of this book was a decision that the Modern Language Association's Commission on the Status of Women in the Profession made in 1986 to sponsor a forum called "Politics and the Discipline" at the December 1987 convention. Little did we know then that Allan Bloom's *The Closing of the American Mind* and E. D. Hirsch's *Cultural Literacy,* both published by commercial presses in 1987, would bring the politics of knowledge to the general public and generate loud debate over the value of reforms instituted by feminists and left-wing critics of the disciplines during the seventies. We did know, however, that the New Right had become a powerful force not only in religion and government but also in education, and we wished to address the dangers of the movement to our own discipline and to intellectual and cultural life in America.

At the forum in San Francisco, Henry Louis Gates, Jr., Annette Kolodny, Ellen Messer-Davidow, and Catharine Stimpson, the four participants, discussed the ways in which right-wing politics has affected literary criticism and theory, research, and higher education in the past ten years. Their papers—some of them slightly expanded—are included in this volume along with talks by Gerald Graff and Paul Lauter, who also oppose the "back-to-basics" agenda, and by Ana Celia Zentella, a Puerto Rican linguist and feminist, who has spoken out against the English-only movement. All of these critics wish to call attention to the ideological nature of our discourse.

Many people deserve mention for recognizing the importance of relating national politics in the 1980s to changes in our discipline. So I would like to thank the MLA Commission on the Status of Women in the Profession, which sponsored the forum and its accompanying workshops and related sessions.

Those on the CSWP during this period were Shari Benstock, Isabelle de Courtivron, Moira Ferguson, Nellie McKay, Valerie Miner, Dolores Palomo, Diana Rebolledo, Eve Sedgwick, Valerie Smith, Elaine Upton-Pugh, Diana Vélez, Phyllis Franklin, and myself. And I would like to thank Karen Orchard, associate director of the University of Georgia Press, for her guidance in assembling this book and Nancy Holmes for her excellent copyediting.

Literature,
Language,
and
Politics

The Two Criticisms

Structure, Lingo, and Power in the Discourse of Academic Humanists

Paul Lauter

In October 1966 the Johns Hopkins Humanities Center was the site of an international symposium titled "The Languages of Criticism and the Sciences of Man." The name of the symposium expresses part of its ambition: to model literary criticism on certain "scientific" paradigms. In particular, the meeting was designed to explore the implications of structuralist thinking—and especially that of Continental scholars—on "critical methods in humanistic and social sciences." Whatever the organizers may have meant by "humanistic . . . sciences," and whatever the value of the conference in examining structuralist thought, as it turned out the symposium will be remembered historically, if at all, as the beginning of *post*-structuralist analysis in the United States. At the conference Jacques Derrida made his American debut, delivering a critique of structuralism whose title, "Structure, Sign, and Play in the Discourse of the Human Sciences," embodied many of the terms and concepts that have since characterized academic criticism in this country.[1] In the two decades after that Baltimore conference, some version of Derridean analysis—call it deconstructionist, speculative, formalist, or, my preference, "ludic"—has become increasingly central to the practice of literary study, at least as it is carried out in the influential academic towers of New Haven and its suburbs across the land.

A few months before this event in 1966, and I dare say unnoted at that conference, Stokely Carmichael had posed a new slogan for what had been considered the "civil rights movement." Carmichael had been arrested by Greenwood, Mississippi, police when, on June 16, participants in the march named after James Meredith had attempted to erect their tents at a local black school. During that evening's rally, Carmichael angrily asserted that blacks had obtained nothing in years of asking for freedom; "what we gonna start saying now," he insisted, is " 'black power.' " The crowd responded immediately to those words, chanting its "black power" response to Carmichael's call. In the months that followed, Carmichael and other leaders of the movement enunciated their conception of black power. In one moment of rhetorical fervor Carmichael asserted, "when you talk of black power, you talk of building a movement that will smash everything Western civilization has created."[2]

One other 1966 event brought questions of power and politics directly into sanctified academic halls: at the University of Chicago that year, Naomi Weisstein, a psychologist, taught an undergraduate course on women.[3] It was probably not the first, for others had been developed at free universities and similar institutions. But Weisstein's course may have represented the initial effort at converting the as-yet-unformed ideas of the women's liberation movement into curricular terms.

Now it may seem "ludic" indeed to speak within two pages of structuralism and Black Power, of a Johns Hopkins symposium and an undergraduate course on women, of Jacques Derrida, Stokely Carmichael, and Naomi Weisstein. But I want to suggest that the Johns Hopkins symposium, on the one hand, and, on the other, the Black Power march and the course on women may serve well as symbols of two alternative movements in contemporary literary study. I want to sketch out these significantly distinct forms of critical and teaching activity. And because I speak as a partisan, from within one, I want to say candidly from the start that my intention is to promote a particular outlook on the work we do as English teachers and scholars. It is my view that, especially at this historic moment of reform in American higher education, the power exercised by formalist, ludic modes of criticism in American academic circles is peculiarly pernicious and needs consciously to be contested. I will ask that readers join in the contest, but in citing the Meredith march, Carmichael, and Black Power at the outset, I wish to suggest that the contest is at its heart political as well as cultural, social as well as literary, and that the choices involved are as conflicting today—if not as brutally explicit— as they were on that steaming Greenwood night twenty-two years ago.

The two forms of literary study I wish to distinguish are, first, the various formalist or speculative criticisms, heavily indebted to Continental philosophy, deeply concerned with questions of epistemology, and practiced primarily at a set of graduate institutions in the United States and France; and, second, what I shall term "canonical" criticism, focused on how we construct our syllabi and anthologies, on the roots of our systems of valuation, on how we decide what's important for us to teach and for our students to learn, or at least to read.

I am not proposing that the existence of two such alternative forms of criticism distinguishes our time, or that this distinction is especially original. Laurence Lerner, for example, argues that "the division between those who see literature as a more or less self-contained system, and those who see it as interacting with real, extra-literary experience . . . is a profoundly important one—perhaps as important as any other . . ."[4] But he goes on to dismiss the difference as not useful to critical practice. I think that this distinction, however philosophically naïve Lerner's statement of it may be, is the most recent version of an old contention between what we might call aesthetic (or formalist) and moral (or what I will call canonical) approaches to texts. Unlike Lerner, I believe that understanding the history of these differing forms of literary study in the past three decades is crucial to perceiving where we are now as literary people and where we might want to go. Consequently, I want to begin with some admittedly crude distinctions and then proceed to refine them by placing my two critical paradigms in the specific historical contexts represented by the Johns Hopkins symposium, on the one hand, and the Black Power march and women's studies course, on the other.

What I am calling aesthetic or formalist criticism began in our time by viewing literature as in some sense a special kind of discourse,[5] composed by specially talented individuals called "poets" (and, more recently, "theorists") and offering unique forms of knowledge or experience, distinct from those presented by science or journalism or rhetoric (propaganda). It has ended by absorbing into this segregated aesthetic domain every kind of text.[6] The other, moral or canonical criticism, has seen literature as one among many forms of discourse whose objective is to move, to enlighten, or perhaps to mystify human beings. The first maintains that while we might, in Emerson's language, be "the richer" for the poet's knowledge, poetic expression involves no necessary extension into the world, that indeed literature has no designs on our conduct, that a poem—to take this position to its familiar New Critical extreme—"should not mean but be." The other, the moral view, emphasizes the impact of literary works on how we conduct our lives, how we live within, extend or restrict, and develop the communities which give our lives meaning. Literary commentators, in the aesthetic vision, have constituted a kind of priesthood of the craft, performing a task of formal analysis given sanction by the special importance of poetry itself or by the notion that texts alone are in some sense "real." The moral practitioner emerges rather more as a teacher, the value of her or his pedagogy affirmed, if at all, by its social consequences. The universe of aesthetic discourse, at least as it has come to be defined by academic critics and by poets like Wallace Stevens as well, is thus distinct, removed, even self-enclosed, a singular place where initiates speak mainly to one another in special languages, hermeneutics, and discuss texts in modes whose authenticity seems measured by their density. In the universe of moralist discourse persons as diverse as Stokely Carmichael, Naomi Weisstein, and Michel Foucault speak—indeed, often shout—in what appears at first as a babel of expedient tongues joined in a contest for priority.

The division I am charting may be illustrated by an anecdote—one which, incidentally, suggests that the sides cannot easily be ranged along the usual Left/Right political spectrum. In about 1970, a group of scholars approached the Modern Language Association with the proposal to hold a "Marxist forum" at the annual convention in New York. Having been refused, they turned to the Radical Caucus of the MLA, an officially recognized "allied organization," which agreed to sponsor the event. Plans for the forum eventually generated considerable conflict between Radical Caucus members and Marxist scholars, largely because the latter's plans called for all the presenters to be white and male. Still, when the event began, the crowd was so large that the walls of the ballroom had to be opened to accommodate the press. By the second highly theoretical paper, however, fully half those who had come were out in the hall, noisily renewing old acquaintances, discovering what others were doing, hatching plans for political actions during the convention—to the intense disgust of those within the hall. And while the Radical Caucus continued to sponsor the forum for a year or two more, until a separate Marxist Literary Group was established, conflict between the groups became, if anything, even more intense than their quarrels with the MLA. "Academic Marxologists," one side sneered; "mindless activists," the other retorted. To be sure, it was a contentious, sectarian time on the Left, and personalities as always played a role in exaggerating this division; but at heart, I think, the groups had significantly differing agendas. One sought primarily to legitimate Marxist theory as a framework for approaching texts; the other, to open the profession and thus the culture to what it saw as fundamental change.

Of course, there is no necessary connection between what I have here termed aestheticism as an approach to literature and the institutionalization of this form of criticism in the academy. Nor has aestheticism always faced inward. Indeed, more than once—in Shelley, for example, or in Wilde—aestheticism has emerged as a revolutionary thrust against prior moralizing styles. But in *our* time aesthetic or formalist criticism seems to me to have embodied not only many of the virtues of speculative thought first demonstrated by Plato but all the limiting features of Plato's Academy as well: its symbolic location in an Athenian suburb, its emphasis upon abstraction and its contempt for the rhetoricians of Isocrates' school for politics, and of course its master's devotion to publishing.

His master, as we know, perished. Plato was out of town at the time. No surprise, as one of my colleagues at San Jose State commented, since Western civilization has been notoriously hard on its teachers. I will return to that observation shortly, but first I want to follow more carefully the emergence of formalism as the most privileged form of literary discourse in the American academy.

Book titles provide us with something of a superficial but still useful set of guideposts to the history of American literary criticism over the past half-century. Cleanth Brooks's *The Well-Wrought Urn*[7] may be taken to represent New Critical practice at its best. Brooks focuses, as the title suggests, on the work itself: its character ("urn" rather than beaker or crock), its quality ("well-wrought"), and his metaphysical sources of poetic value (Donne's "The Canonization"). He makes little reference to the social or cultural circumstances that determined the potter's clay, available glazes, and decorative modes. Or, indeed, who might a potter be. While we are all indebted to, or at least influenced by, the habits of mind established by Brooks and his colleagues—close reading of texts, sensitivity to such qualities as ambiguity, irony, paradox—New Criticism represented an elitist, if unsystematic, mode of critical judgment and worked with a narrow set of texts amenable to its analytic methods. Northrop Frye, whose work at once looks back to the practical criticism of Brooks and forward to the more systematic efforts of structuralism, borrows his central, taxonomic metaphor from biology: *Anatomy of Criticism*.[8] The metaphor proposes a closed, if organic and growing, domain for criticism, in which the critic's role is to identify the distinctive features and underlying functions of each part of the literary body and to discern how they may be related both to one another and to the underlying mythoi which Frye sees, like genetic determinants, at the center of all literary texts.

Beginning in the late sixties, and with increasing rapidity, various forms of structuralism—those, for example, associated with Roland Barthes[9] and with Marxists like Fredric Jameson[10]—emerged as the dominant critical paradigms, only to be contested in short order by bewildering varieties of post-structuralist theorizing. The title of Harold Bloom's early work, *The Anxiety of Influence*,[11] emphasizes a psychological category as key to a viable theory of poetry and collapses history into the set of pressures imposed by strong poetic predecessors upon every individual practitioner. One can go on in this mode: Paul de Man's *Blindness and Insight* suggests something of the ludic, paradoxical quality of much recent theoretical writing, whereas Geoffrey Hartman's *Criticism in the Wilderness*[12] mirrors its somewhat pessimistic tone and its claims to social marginality. But my intention is not to impose such reductive characterizations on these works; rather, I want to suggest something of their variety in order to ask whether such disparate projects have anything in common.

There seem to me two ways of answering that question. One, via philosophy, is to ask whether these modes of critical writing share certain characteristics or concerns or assumptions, whether they have any common essence.
I will speak briefly to that in a moment. But my major interest is to see
whether these varied critical styles are radically alike in terms of the roles they
have played and the practical effects they have had on our profession and on
the institutions, English departments, colleges and universities, in which we
work. As for the first, Frank Lentricchia has tracked the "repeated and often
extremely subtle denial of history" in the work especially of American theorists who came, to use the title of his book, *After the New Criticism*.[13] In
using the words *formalist* and *aesthetic* to name these varied styles of criticism, I wish to point to their pervasive effort to separate literary texts (whatever might be meant by "literary") as well as critical acts from history, their
tendency to ignore the particular roles their work is playing in educational
institutions and in society, and their consequent tendency to turn the domain of
literature—again in Lentricchia's words—into a "vast, enclosed textual and
semantic preserve" (p. xiii). "Formalist" suggests that the whole enterprise of
literary theorizing subsists behind dense academic walls, where de Man spoke
only to Heidegger, and Heidegger spoke only to God. Whereas theoretical
criticism can be challenged on its own philosophical grounds, as indeed
Lentricchia partly does, that seems to me to offer no exit from the "Wilderness" where Geoffrey Hartman has most recently located criticism. And
worse, it seems to accelerate the centrifugal force that continues to move
literary study to the very fringe of college education. We need, rather, to
understand why speculative criticism developed such an enormous vogue in
the late sixties and seventies, why its practitioners have come to be dominant
figures in the American literary establishment, why its terminology slips so
trippingly from the tongues of serious graduate students, why job lists multi-
ply calls for practitioners of "theory," and, finally, why it has spun so increasingly into irrelevance to the concerns we face every day as teachers and
as intellectuals.

I want then to ask whether the rise of formalist theory—whatever precisely
one means by that term[14]—as the dominant mode of literary discourse in
American academic circles can be understood in the specific historical context
of the last twenty-five years. I also want to ask whether formalist criticism
taken as a whole has played an identifiable institutional role and had specific
impact upon university education. Here my initial symbols—the Johns Hopkins symposium, the Black Power march, and the women's studies course—
again become helpful. New Criticism emerged in the 1920s and 1930s
precisely as the social authority of those who came to practice it was being
undermined. Similarly, the cultural and social authority of those of us presum-

ably entrusted with sustaining and transmitting the heritage of Western civilization was sharply being challenged at the end of the 1960s, as Stokely Carmichael's comments about Black Power illustrate, and as the subsequent disruptions of normal academic life on most campuses were shortly to dramatize. Not only were we accused of irrelevance in our provincial pursuit of ironies, myths, and publication, but we were charged with leading humane study up academic labyrinths at the very moment its insights were needed to negotiate the multiplying crises of civil rights, the Vietnam war, continued domestic and colonial poverty, not to speak of the Bomb. In the 1968 charge on the Modern Language Association convention,[15] one could all but hear echoing from the marbled halls of the old Hotel Americana a version of Wordsworth's cry to Milton in the poem "London, 1802": "England hath need of thee: she is a fen / Of stagnant waters." I think the turn to theory was in part a response to such attacks—in certain ways an effort, parallel to that being mounted by some left-wing sects, to apply European intellectual models to intransigent American social issues. In other respects, however, it became little more than a series of linguistic moves whose dominant effect was to sustain academic privilege.

Frye's work, like that of many writers after him, represented a reasonable effort to impose theoretical coherence on the exceedingly miscellaneous practices displayed by literary criticism as it, like academic America generally, dilated wildly through the sixties. Furthermore, new models being created in other disciplines (for example, the structuralism of Levi-Strauss) proved readily adaptable to literary analysis. As the centrality of humane, and especially literary, study eroded, some theorists attempted at first to reprivilege that work by attaching it to these supposedly more scientific paradigms. Thus literary structuralists adapted to their criticism anthropological accounts of social organization and of underlying historical and linguistic patterns. Later, deconstructionist critics attempted to link—or perhaps it might be more accurate to say "transform"—literary study to the presumably more rigorous philosophical styles represented by Derrida and Foucault.

For some younger members of the profession in the early seventies, familiarity with Maitre Jacques, S/Z, or the Frankfurt school offered a powerful tool. At worst, one could deploy modes of analysis, a "text milieu," and a discourse altogether unfamiliar to an older generation of empirical critics; in that alone was power. At best, certain theoretical moves seem to have been as intellectually freeing for some entering graduate work during the Nixon years as participation in the movements for social change of the prior decade was for me and my activist comrades. They undercut the claims to objectivity and disinterested evaluation of texts—or of events—made by those in power. Certain forms of theory demanded the rehistoricizing not only of literary works but of the work of literary people, even as they called into question the relationship between textual depictions and the "realities" of which they were presumed to be accounts. What Lyndon Johnson's "construction" of Vietnam had forced some of us to understand, Derrida on the historical construction of *différance* appears to have opened to others. Further, certain theorists began to break down idealist distinctions between literary and assertedly nonliterary texts, thus opening to study an ever-broadening range of noncanonical works. What theoretical study at its best provided, or at least claimed the ability to provide, was a more self-conscious account of the underlying assumptions we all use in situating the works we read. The theorists, and especially the post-structuralists, said that before we look at the pattern we see on the page, we must examine the glasses through which we necessarily perceive it and which may, in fact, have given a coherent shape to an otherwise undifferentiated blob of ink. And thus a new generation of critics has come to study the lenses of perception, together with—often in place of—the texts perceived.

For all that, theory as a mode of literary discourse (or, as I would describe it, a maneuver in academic political rhetoric) has primarily succeeded in re-establishing academic privilege—ironically, not for the study of literature in the academy, but for those who practice theory within the literary profession. In fact, as English departments have lost ground through the last decade and a half, the practical effect of the privileging of theorists has been to deepen the abyss—and also to widen the pay differential—between those who dwell in the towers of academe and those who inhabit its trenches. All one needs to see are the salaries paid the new specialist in theory at Texas and the often older teacher of freshman English at San Jose State. *Différance* indeed! In retrospect it should not be surprising that yesterday's theoretical *enfant terrible* so rapidly becomes today's MLA president, or that yesterday's gauntlet becomes today's protector of the most traditional anthologies and curricula. American literary theory has proved remarkably easy to assimilate to the structure of American university life; indeed, it has become a strong reenforcement of existing academic norms. The practice of literary theory in no sense challenges the individualistic, production-oriented forms of the American academy; like other forms of critical production, the work of theorists can easily be measured (so many articles, books, or citations in other works) and displayed to appropriate authorities. And it helps maintain a hierarchical relationship between the privileged discourse of the academy and practical criticism, mainly carried out in the classroom.

In that regard, the obscurity of language which has come to characterize most theoretical writing is no unfortunate accident but rather an essential element. To be sure, as theory has developed over the last decade, its practitioners have with increasing self-consciousness sought originality above all else, at least originality of expression if not always of idea. But the real function of linguistic opacity is little different from that of the Latin scrawls of physicians to pharmacists: keep the unwashed out of the game. If you don't know the values of chips like "extradiscursive formations," "neo-Gramscian framework," "hegemonic discourses," "monologic ideologization," "representational algorithm," you're likely to lose your shirt in the play of discourse. And if a critic wants to "call into question both the economy of identity and the axiology of binarity that underwrites the nomology of identity," who are most of us to ask, "does it matter"? Discussion of complex ideas can, of course, be complicated, and the Derridean play of language and ideas can occasionally be as entertaining as a few moments in a Ping Chong performance. But finally we need to ask about the functions of particular language practices in the American academy. The ostensible political objectives of the essays from which these examples are chosen are quite progressive, but the linguistic style is exclusionary, elitist, and what Raymond Williams has called "dominative"; that is its purpose.

Suiting practice to theory, moreover, formalism in any of its modes has sustained a fifty-year tradition of privileging in literary study "major" works by "major" authors. If you apply what I like to call the "index test" to the work of the leading theoretical critics, you obtain figures like the following: Paul de Man's *Blindness and Insight* refers to 139 men and, passingly, to two women; Hartman's relatively more popular essays in *The Fate of Reading*[16] mention 232 men, many frequently, and eleven women. The notion that the universe of academic discourse is a male (and not so incidentally white and European) world is thus strongly reenforced. One looks through such pages almost in vain for any account of W. E. B. DuBois, Virginia Woolf, C. L. R. James. It is then no long step to the position taken by Howard Felperin in his 1985 defense of theoretical criticism, disingenuously titled *Beyond Deconstruction*. Felperin acknowledges that "the question of the canon goes to the heart of the institution's peculiar existence." He continues:

> Just as a certain kind of writing, the kind that has come to be known as "literature," is inconceivable without authorship, so the institutional study of that writing is inconceivable without a canon. Without a canon, a corpus or cynosure of exemplary texts, there can be no interpretive community. . . . The argument for a canon derives, that is, not from the importance of our reading the *right* texts, whatever our criteria of rectitude (moral, political, historical, rhetorical), but from the necessity of our reading the *same* texts, or enough of the same texts, to enable the discourse of the interpretive community to go on.[17]

Thus Felperin, asserting the primacy of maintaining theoretical discourse, argues for a "conservative approach" to canon formation. "Let us," he quotes Keats, "have the old poets and Robin Hood," and he comments: "While

'Robin Hood' may assume the guise of popular, women's, or ethnic literature in response to special historical interests, it seems unlikely that a fully institutional canon could ever be formed out of them, simply because the interests they represent are special or sectarian, and hence, exclusive" (p. 48). It amazes me how a critic trained in the tactics of deconstructive textualism can so blithely imply the supposedly universal character of the rather special interests represented by the traditional canon, and embodied in the indices upon which I reported above. Indeed, Felperin's comments dramatize why criticism and teaching that cohere around the issue of the canon lead in directions radically different from the *cul-de-sac* in which theory has left us.

It is not that theoretical critics are dull or malicious individuals; on the contrary, those of us who teach writing and courses in critical thinking have a good deal to learn from people like Foucault and Hartman. But the institutional roles played by American theorists in the last two decades have been decidedly retrogressive and have helped deepen the crisis of the humanities to which former Secretary of Education William Bennett has, however wrongheadedly, given notoriety.[18]

The distinctive qualities of canonical criticism may come sharply into relief if we contrast it with the kind of formalism I have been describing. I want to outline the project of canonical criticism and suggest three stages in its development. As my signposts—the Meredith march and the Weisstein course— suggest, the roots of this form of literary activity reach deeply into the movements for social change of the 1960s and 1970s. Indeed, it would not be too much to say that canonical criticism constitutes a part of a broader effort to reconstruct our society, and particularly our educational institutions, on a more democratic and equitable basis. It emerges from a fundamental perception: that curricula, reading lists, degree requirements, and anthologies institutionalize ideas about what is important, *whose* experiences and artistic expressions are to be valued. As affirmative action in personnel procedures reflected the efforts of minorities and white women to penetrate and reshape American institutional life, so canonical criticism as it emerged two decades ago was at heart an effort to open up literary study and to reconstruct it on new, more inclusive bases.

For example, if we strip away from Carmichael's exposition of "black power" some of its rhetorical vehemence, we will quickly see that the slogan significantly represented for him an effort "to reclaim our [black] history and our [black] identity," that it named a "struggle for the right to create our own terms to define ourselves and our relationship to society, and to have these terms recognized."[19] In such a struggle, education and culture necessarily played critical roles in overturning the old saying, embodied in most 1950s curricula, "out of sight, out of mind." To place the work and life of women and minority men into the curriculum *was* in important ways to make them a presence in educational institutions. To be sure, if curricula and other forms of institutional life were so conceived and so structured as to exclude the history, identity, and achievements—not to speak of the physical presence—of minorities or of white women, then indeed academic practice and organization would have to be reconstructed. And since privilege and power are not lightly surrendered, since what we understand as norms are not quickly transformed, Carmichael's operative verb might indeed emerge as *smash:* "smash everything Western civilization has created," that is, the exclusive construction of culture—or of philosophy—expressed in most Western civilization courses and similar curricula before the late 1960s.

I am not proposing that Carmichael's rhetoric or the intellectual processes it implies were comforting or even compatible with academic norms. But I do want to make two things clear: first, the issue of the canon—what we study, what we conceive as significant, not just in literature but in almost every discipline—has always arisen from efforts to redress social wrongs. And second, debate over canonical issues deeply affects the ways people conceive, regulate, and change their lives. In other words, the problem of the canon will persist so long as we see education, and more particularly cultural practice and study, as fundamentally related to social justice, or even to the evolution of human communities.

These points may be clarified by considering some of the significant texts of early canonical criticism. I would cite first the series called Female Studies, published in the late sixties and early seventies by KNOW, Inc. and The Feminist Press. These volumes collected syllabi and course materials from the first practitioners of women's studies in many disciplines and in a variety of academic settings. They were by nature collective rather than individualistic, displaying the scholarship and pedagogical practices of many teachers. They emerged, of course, from the experience of *teachers* and spoke to practical classroom problems: what texts to use, how to organize them, how such choices were related both to changing student populations and to traditionally defined academic structures, like departments and course requirements. Whereas such volumes were enormously important "contributions to knowledge," that phrase was not conceived by contributors to the books in traditional terms. A new syllabus, in other words, often reflects an intense scholarly enterprise and generally new research as well; however, it is conceived and presented not as a permanent cultural monument but rather as an educational tool that will, in time, be superseded. We write our most precious conceptions onto the ditto-master for distribution, and next year we use the surplus copies for scrap. We are like the Japanese fisherman who inscribed his poems on scrolls, which he then necessarily used to wrap the fish he sold.

Among those concerned primarily with African-American literature, canonical criticism in the late sixties and early seventies often emerged in the form of anthologies and collections of essays by different hands. To be sure, the appearance of such books primarily revealed publishers' judgments that black literature was being taught and might also sell in the general literary market. But these volumes also represented a means by which black artists and critics expressed ideas about what constitutes the distinctive canon of African-American literary art. For example, most of the 1968 anthologies—Abraham Chapman's *Black Voices,* James A. Emanuel and Theodore L. Gross's *Dark Symphony,* and Amiri Baraka and Larry Neal's *Black Fire—* contain both belles lettres and social and political criticism (the distinction is not emphasized) in proportions markedly different from those which characterize traditional, dominantly white anthologies. Similarly, Paul Bremen's *You Better Believe It* (1973) includes poetry from Africa, the West Indies and the United States, emphasizing the relationships among these, and Stephen Henderson's *Understanding the New Black Poetry: Black Speech and Black Music as Poetic References* (1973) includes songs and black folk rhymes, as well as formal poetry, to represent the range of black poetic forms that need to be taught and studied by critics. Addison Gayle's widely read *The Black Aesthetic* (1971) and his *Black Expression* (1969) also include essays on music and art, and on folk culture, as well as on formal literature, thus offering what might be termed an interdisciplinary perspective on African-American art. That five of my seven titles use the word *black* (and one *dark*) also suggests a central concern these books share with Carmichael: to define what it means to be black in late twentieth-century America.

As it emerged in the late sixties and early seventies, then, canonical criticism focused first on practical matters like organizing syllabi and making otherwise forgotten texts and authors available, especially for classrooms. These pedagogical and archaeological tasks continue, as various publications in 1985 illustrate: *First Feminists: British Women Writers, 1578–1799,* edited by Moira Ferguson; *Provisions: A Reader from 19th Century American Women,* edited by Judith Fetterley; *Hidden Hands: An Anthology of American Women Writers, 1790–1870,* edited by Lucy Freibart and Barbara White; and Sandra Gilbert and Susan Gubar's massive *Norton Anthology of Literature by Women.* Alongside this work, often in fact as a part of it, have developed certain other strands of critical practice which I wish to identify and trace.

Beginning in 1966, texts previously ignored in syllabi and anthologies began to be read in and out of the classroom. I refer to works like Zora Neale Hurston's *Their Eyes Were Watching God,* Rebecca Harding Davis's "Life in the Iron Mills," Frederick Douglass's autobiographical *Narrative,* and Margaret Fuller's *Woman in the Nineteenth Century.* At the same time, significant contemporary works that drew on ethnic traditions began to achieve a wide audience, works such as Rudolfo Anaya's *Bless Me, Ultima,* Leslie Silko's *Ceremony,* and Maxine Hong Kingston's *The Woman Warrior.* More recently, too, critics have begun to reexamine whole bodies of distinctive works—for example, the poetry of female modernists or the 1850s fiction of American women. In many ways, all these works fell outside the existing accounts of American or British literary traditions, and so there began to develop a second, *synthetic* stage of canonical criticism. Rather early, black critics like Stephen Henderson, Addison Gayle, and Houston Baker[20] mounted a project to define the particular qualities which constitute an African-American tradition in American writing. Similarly, feminist critics like Ellen Moers, Elaine Showalter, Sandra Gilbert and Susan Gubar, and Barbara Christian began to describe dominantly female (and, except in Christian's work, largely white) traditions in literature,[21] as well as woman-centered cultural networks such as the late-nineteenth-century group that cohered around Sarah Orne Jewett and Annie Fields.[22] The efforts of African-Americans to define a peculiarly "black" content in their writing and to trace its impact in the historical worlds inhabited by black people have recently been criticized by more formalist commentators.[23] But such complaints really miss the point of what these early canonical critics were about: their problem was less to define the underlying structural principles of writing by black Americans or women than to seek out the ways in which such writing played roles in the "struggle for the right to create our own terms to define ourselves . . . and to have these terms recognized," to use Carmichael's phraseology once again. The major cultural task of canonical criticism in the late sixties and seventies, its second stage, was to "define ourselves" and then to force into literary consciousness ("have these terms recognized") texts previously conceived as peripheral—texts that illustrated a whole cultural tradition and thus the life of a marginalized group or people. Establishing such traditions not only demonstrated the extent and range of African-American or female cultures but also showed the critical *difference* inherent in such cultures. That presented a direct challenge to the ideology of academic formalism, which rejected the idea that literature might legitimately play such social roles and which, at some level, continued to assert universality, not difference, as fundamental to literary value. It may be that the earliest black critics can be reproved for their limited accounts of how literature plays roles in the world and about the character of an African-American tradition; if we recall, however, how fully formalist criticism and McCarthyite politics had buried ideas about the social functions of writing, we will regard the work of early black critics as a heroic effort to reconstruct a lost critical tradition.

These canonical critics recognized that underlying the questions of what we teach and to whom, what we anthologize, publish, and write about, are ideas about what we value and why. Standards of value tend to be self-perpetuating: we are taught to seek the works that illustrate the qualities we value; we learn to value the qualities that characterize such works. Responding to the social movements of the sixties, and to the first stage of discovery of "new" texts, these critics demonstrated precisely the process of canonical change described by T. S. Eliot in "Tradition and the Individual Talent": the "modification" of the "ideal order" of the "existing monuments" of culture. In that process, we began to recognize that touchstones of literary value are not, in fact, inscribed on tablets at all but are mutable constructs devised at particular times by particular people with particular aspirations and constraints. We saw that such standards change, that they are differently held by distinct communities; indeed, by virtue of our participation in such diverse communities—of nationality, race, sex, profession, institution—we ourselves may maintain conflicting sets of values and thus of literary standards.

When we begin to acknowledge how distinct value systems are embodied in diverse cultural assumptions and forms (the third stage of canonical criticism where we find ourselves today), we begin to deconstruct the underlying assumptions of received systems of evaluation. It seems to me that Jane Tompkins's 1985 book, *Sensational Designs,* [24] represents this kind of cultural work. On the one hand, Tompkins cuts through the mystifications that have been used to certify particular writers, like Hawthorne, as "classics"; on the other, she illuminates the social and literary values that define the importance of marginalized writers, like Stowe and Susan Warner. What Tompkins's project amounts to, what the project of canonical criticism now implies, is a radical reassessment of literary standards and therefore of social and political values.

If I have correctly mapped these alternative parabolas of recent critical history, what do the curves imply for our practice, in teaching as well as in our professional and institutional lives?

In teaching (and in writing as well) I think we should consider adopting what I like to call a comparative strategy. That is, we might set established and nontraditional texts side by side to note their similarities and differences with respect to a wide variety of features, including subject matter, language, structure, imagery, and even effect upon our students. In a senior seminar at San Jose State, for example, we studied Hawthorne's *The House of the Seven Gables* with Stowe's *The Minister's Wooing,* Twain's *Pudd'nhead Wilson* with Charles Chesnutt's *The Marrow of Tradition,* Anderson's *Winesburg, Ohio* with Jewett's *The Country of the Pointed Firs,* and Hemingway's *A Farewell to Arms* with Hurston's *Their Eyes Were Watching God.* I find this strategy enormously revealing—of traditional and "new" works, of the periods in which they were written, of assumptions we bring to them, and of how we learn from books.

To take a brief example, both the Hawthorne and the Stowe novels exemplify characteristics of the mid-nineteenth-century romance. They set the power of love, and especially of the innocent American girl, against the burdens of history, particularly the legacies of Puritanism. But they offer very different centers of value, narrative strategies, and understandings about the force of history. In a certain sense, history does not exist for Hawthorne, as for many of his Romantic contemporaries; it simply reflects, generation by generation, the repeated operation of Pyncheon greed and Maule's curse. His interest lies in the impact of such persisting forces on the aesthetic temperament, embodied in Clifford. Thus Hawthorne's characters can emerge from the closed circle of essentially repeated events only by the unconvincing *dei ex machina* which kill off Judge Pyncheon and his son, hitch Phoebe and Holgrave, and thus permit the happy ending commanded by sentimental tradition.

For Stowe, the legacy of Puritanism is more complex than repeated instances of "sin and sorrow." The Reverend Mr. Hopkins is a man of intensely lived moral power, especially in his active condemnation of slaveholding, but he is also blinkered by his devotion to a heartless metaphysical system. The historical issue for Stowe, which bears directly upon the conduct of life in mid-nineteenth-century America, is how to sustain the moral seriousness and fervor of Puritanism without its terrorizing theology. The marriage that celebrates the ending of her book presents her symbolic solution to this problem and also satisfies the period's conventions. Hawthorne's work is a sustained, I would suggest an enclosed, meditation upon aestheticism outside history (which may be part of its attraction to aesthetically minded literary critics). Stowe's is, I think, an effort to translate the values of a particular era into actions comprehensible to a contemporary audience. My concern here is not to prefer one mode over the other but to propose how viewing them together reveals the qualities of both—their deep similarities and differences—and also clarifies our own ideas about literary structure and function.

One could illustrate at some length the virtues of a comparative approach to studying literature. But I wish to conclude by connecting what I have written about two conflicting modes of criticism back to the real political and institutional worlds in which we teach and live.

As we all know, studies about higher education have multiplied these last few years even more rapidly than intellectual styles in Paris. These studies say to us: "revive the art of teaching, especially in the humanities." Some, like William Bennett, bid us return to the traditional canon of the 1950s, the Western classics plus Martin Luther King, Jr., for color. Others tell us, like the organizers of that Johns Hopkins symposium in 1966, to make the study of literature more systematic, more philosophically grounded,[25] and thus more credible. Both these notions, in my view, lead to blank walls—at least so far as teaching is concerned. We cannot go back to the 1950s illusion that this is a homogeneous society without conflict, where ideology is at an end and difference a threat. Nor is it sensible to pursue theories of literature or of "texts" down obscure corridors ever more remote from the lives of our students.

In the final analysis, literature is important to read and study because it opens life to us, and to the people we teach—life in all its contradiction and pleasure, in its absurdity and pain, in its aspiration and, so very profoundly in poetry, its accomplishment. I have urged canonical criticism on my readers. In opening the canon, the curriculum, the classroom, we open our students' lives to Frederick Douglass struggling from the pit of slavery and contemplating the role of force in his liberation, to Jewett's Mrs. Todd drawing us toward human community in the corners where it survives, to Tillie Olsen's Eva in death preserving the shards of revolution through decades of riddles, to Silko's Indian veteran, Tayo, opening himself to the power of his heritage. We open our students to the power of language, as a craft and as an instrument.

To the extent that we bring the multiplicity of our cultur*es* and our literatur*es* into our classrooms, to the extent that those classrooms pulse with the languages and lives we read, we will lead criticism out of the wilderness where it has wandered these forty years. And in that way, I believe, we will begin to restore to its central place in collegiate study the life of the humanities.[26]

Notes

1 For an account of this symposium see Frank Lentricchia, *After the New Criticism* (Chicago: University of Chicago Press, 1980), pp. 157–62.

2 For an account of the Meredith march and the origins of the Black Power slogan see Clayborn Carson, *In Struggle: SNCC and the Black Awakening of the 1960s* (Cambridge: Harvard University Press, 1981), pp. 209–10.

3 See Sara Evans, *Personal Politics: The Roots of Women's Liberation in the Civil Rights Movement and the New Left* (New York: Vintage, 1980), pp. 185–86.

4 Introduction to *Reconstructing Literature* (Totowa, N.J.: Barnes and Noble, 1983), p. 6.

5 Howard Felperin argues that "all of the dominant schools of contemporary criticism—marxism, structuralism, and deconstruction—have converged upon" the "myth" of a "privileged literary language," "dismantling it of its idealist and

metaphysical yearnings and trappings, its Arnoldian inheritance of displaced religion" (*Beyond Deconstruction* [Oxford: Clarendon Press, 1985], p. 11). Yet the concept continually and perversely reemerges. For example, Paul de Man argues that "literature, unlike everyday language, begins on the far side of this knowledge [that "sign and meaning can never coincide"]; it is the only form of language free from the fallacy of unmediated expression. All of us know this, although we know it in the misleading way of a wishful assertion of the opposite. Yet the truth emerges in the foreknowledge we possess of the true nature of literature when we refer to it as *fiction*" (*Blindness and Insight* [New York: Oxford University Press, 1981], p. 17). The obvious problem in de Man's formulation is in his dichotomizing "literature" and "everyday language" and in his privileging "literature" as "the only form of language." In truth, literary and everyday language are radically alike; both involve—more and less—the construction and recommendation of "fictions," the use of images, the mobilization of rhetorics, and the like. In fact, a major cause for failure in the teaching of literature is our habit of erecting linguistic and formal walls between it and our students' use of language.

6 See Robert Scholes, "Some Problems in Current Graduate Programs in English," *Profession 87*, p. 40: "This second reduction in our field left behind only poetics (and its handmaiden, philology, which has since been dismissed or relegated to the basement). Free to concentrate exclusively on the poetic or literary side of English textuality, we were led, inevitably, to a greater and greater degree of formalism in literary studies; to New Criticism, to the Chicago school of generic criticism, later on to structuralism, and finally to deconstruction—which is the aestheticizing of all discourse, the denial that any really persuasive, or informational, or speculative discourse can exist."

7 *The Well-Wrought Urn* (New York: Harcourt, Brace and World, 1947).

8 *Anatomy of Criticism: Four Essays* (New York: Atheneum, 1967).

9 See, for example, *Mythologies*, translated by Annette Lavers (New York: Hill and Wang, 1972), and *S/Z*, translated by Richard Howard (New York: Hill and Wang, 1974).

10 See *The Prison-House of Language: A Critical Account of Structuralism and Russian Formalism* (Princeton: Princeton University Press, 1972).

11 *The Anxiety of Influence: A Theory of Poetry* (New York: Oxford University Press, 1973).

12 *Criticism in the Wilderness: The Study of Literature Today* (New Haven: Yale University Press, 1980).

13 Lentricchia, p. xiii.

14 Theory is, as Jonathan Culler points out, virtually a nickname for a variety of writings that, in the American academy, fall outside the prior domains of English or philosophy or the empirical social sciences as they are generally practiced. See *On Deconstruction: Theory and Criticism after Structuralism* (Ithaca: Cornell University Press, 1982), pp. 8–10. In a strict sense, theoretical writing simply concerns the assumptions (about language, the relationships of signifier and signified, the binary structure of most Western thought, the relations of culture to class-

conflict) we all use in thinking and writing about literature, or about anything else that provides us with a text or subject. In practice, however, the looser sense of the term prevails.

15 For an account of these events see Louis Kampf and Paul Lauter, introduction to *The Politics of Literature* (New York: Pantheon, 1972).

16 Chicago: University of Chicago Press, 1975.

17 *Beyond Deconstruction,* pp. 46–47.

18 See "To Reclaim a Legacy: A Report of the Humanities in Higher Education," National Endowment for the Humanities, November 1984; and my critique of Bennett's ideas in "Looking a Gift Horse in the Mouth," *San Jose Studies* 12 (Winter 1986): 6–19.

19 Cited in Carson, *In Struggle,* p. 216.

20 Stephen Henderson, *Understanding the New Black Poetry* (New York: Morrow, 1972); Addison Gayle, ed., *The Black Aesthetic* (Garden City, N.Y.: Anchor, 1972); Houston Baker, *Long Black Song: Essays in Black American Literature and Culture* (Charlottesville: University of Virginia, 1972).

21 Ellen Moers, *Literary Women: The Great Writers* (Garden City, N.Y.: Doubleday, 1976); Elaine Showalter, *A Literature of Their Own: British Women Novelists from Brontë to Lessing* (Princeton: Princeton University Press, 1978); Sandra M. Gilbert and Susan Gubar, *The Madwoman in the Attic: The Woman Writer and the Nineteenth-Century Literary Imagination* (New Haven: Yale University Press, 1979); Barbara Christian, *Black Women Novelists: The Development of a Tradition, 1892–1976* (Westport: Greenwood, 1980).

More recent works have begun further to define a parallel, largely separate, but sometimes related tradition among black women writers. Among these works are Mary Helen Washington, *Invented Lives* (Garden City, N.Y.: Anchor, 1987), Hazel Carby, *Reconstructing Womanhood* (New York: Oxford, 1987), and Elizabeth Ammons, "New Literary History: Edith Wharton and Jessie Redmon Fauset," *College Literature* 14 (1987): 207–18.

22 See Josephine Donovan, "Annie Adams Fields and Her Network of Influence," *New England Local Color Literature: A Woman's Tradition* (New York: Frederick Ungar, 1983), pp. 38–49.

23 See, for example, Henry Louis Gates, Jr., "Preface to Blackness: Text and Pretext," in *Afro-American Literature: The Reconstruction of Instruction,* ed. Dexter Fisher and Robert B. Stepto (New York: Modern Language Association, 1979), pp. 44–69.

24 *Sensational Designs: The Cultural Work of American Fiction, 1790–1860* (New York: Oxford University Press, 1985).

25 See Scholes, "Some Problems in Current Graduate Programs in English." Scholes's understanding of the range of authors available to study may provide a kind of comic coda to my basic point; he writes: "For our own good as teachers and for the sake of the future of our world, we must learn to engage in critical dialogue not only with such as Jacques Derrida but with such as Jürgen Habermas" (p. 42). Just whose world, one might ask, is it?

26 I wish to express my appreciation for the help of a number of people: Ann Fitzgerald, who encouraged my convictions; the many who heard and commented on this paper when it was first delivered at the 1985 College English Association convention; and Jane Tompkins and Richard Ohmann, both of whom were kind enough to share their criticisms with me in detail. I may not have agreed or learned sufficiently from them, but they immeasurably extended my understanding.

On the Rhetoric of Racism in the Profession

Henry Louis Gates, Jr.

A packed audience sat expectantly at Cornell as a distinguished visitor walked to the podium to share with the audience his latest theory called ethical criticism. His talk was titled "The Ethics of Narration." But owing perhaps to some wit of the local newspaper, which has a black publisher, his talk had been advertised as "The Ethnics of Narration." And so the critic announced to the astonished audience that his talk had been falsely advertised, much to his annoyance, and that those who had come to talk about ethnicity, of all things, most certainly should pick up their coats and notebooks and leave, because he knew nothing about ethnicity. No kidding, I thought to myself. Then the man proceeded to speak to us for over an hour about his view of value, ethics, and Western white literary criticism, in the post-poststructural world, in an Anglo-American manner as ethnic as any of us shall do today. The point was that he did not *know* he was being ethnic, since that word connotes for him some culture of color and not a subdivision of culture itself.

The whole performance recalled to mind Edward Said's recent lecture series at Cornell, a marvelous lecture series soon to be published as a book. During one of Said's lectures I happened to be seated next to a great literary critic. During his third lecture, Said analyzed the theories of several so-called Third World critics, including Fanon, C. L. R. James, Kabrahl, Walter Rodney, and the great Du Bois. Every time Edward said another "strange" name, my colleague would turn to me and ask, first, if I knew his work and, second, whether he was black or white. It happened so often during the talk that my colleague and I arrived at a convenient shorthand. He would raise his eyebrows when he wanted to ask his questions and I would merely turn thumbs up or thumbs down, depending of course on whether African ancestry were involved. I remember thinking at the end of that lecture that we have a very long way to go before older white academic critics begin to read the great theorists of the black traditions in the same way that we read their "theories." This is the topic I wish to discuss.

William Bennett and Allan Bloom, the dynamic duo of the New Cultural Right, have become the easy targets of the Cultural Left, which I am defining here loosely and generously as that uneasy, shifting set of alliances formed by feminist-critics, critics of so-called "minority" discourse, and Marxist and post-structuralist critics generally. Bennett and Bloom are the two symbols of the nostalgic return to what I think of as the "antebellum aesthetic position," when men were men and men were white, when scholar-critics were white men, and when women and persons of color were voiceless, faceless servants and laborers, pouring tea and filling brandy snifters in the board rooms of old boy clubs. Bennett and Bloom have come to play for us the roles that George Wallace and Orville Faubus played for the civil rights movement, or that Nixon and Kissinger played for us during Vietnam—the "feel good" targets, who, despite our internal differences and contradictions, we all love to hate. Of course, when Bennett writes in *To Reclaim a Legacy* that "the core of the American college curriculum—its heart and soul—should be the civilization of the West," and accounts for this so-called civilizing process in terms of the mastery of Matthew Arnold's "the best that has been thought and written" by white males for white males about white males during the past three thousand years, we have little choice but to identify his position as inimical to our best interests and antithetical to the larger socioeconomic changes in the academy for which so many of us have been fighting since the civil rights movement and the protests against the Vietnam war.

Lest we fool ourselves into thinking that opinions such as Bennett's, and the power that he wields, do not have a direct and indirect impact upon our lives and the workplace, we need only recall the racial violence that has swept through our campuses since 1986—at traditionally liberal northern institutions such as Columbia, Chicago, Massachusetts at Amherst, Mount Holyoke, and Smith, and at southern institutions such as Alabama, Texas, and the Citadel. The implicitly racist rhetoric of Bennett's civilizing mission has unfolded precisely as affirmative action programs on campus have become ineffective window-dressing operations, necessary "evils" maintained to preserve the fiction of racial fairness and openness in the truly academic environment, but deprived of the power to enforce their stated principles.

Statistics gathered from the U.S. Census Bureau, the American Council on Education, and the Department of Education's Office of Civil Rights attest to this trend: "Blacks in 1972 constituted 3 percent of the students in four-year institutions. By 1976, however, reflecting the thrust of effective Affirmative Action programs, 1,032,000 blacks made up 9.7 percent of this same college population.

"But, by 1984, just 8 years later, there were only 1,070,000 black students on campus, 8.8 percent of the total. The Census Bureau reports that the number is still declining, down to 1,049,000 in 1985, and still sinking."

The decline in black graduate enrollment is even more alarming. Whereas 5.1 percent of our graduate student population in 1976 was black, only 4.2 percent of all graduate students in 1982 were black, and the percentage of blacks receiving doctoral degrees in all fields has been declining steadily and regularly since 1982. According to the National Research Council, in 1986 alone blacks earned only 820 research doctorates, 26.5 percent fewer than in 1976. More than half of these doctorates (421) were in education or "education-related" fields. We are in the midst of a crisis, the implications of which shall continue to haunt us for generations.

At the same time, there has been a corresponding drop in the number of minority teachers. Blacks, for instance, now constitute only about one percent of all faculty at predominantly white colleges. Despite the strikingly visible increase in black members of the MLA, black and nonblack scholars writing about minority discourse, panels at the MLA annual convention on these topics, and positions available for experts in minority literatures within traditional English and Romance language departments, the MLA and our profession remain overwhelmingly white organizations. All this depressing news unfolds in a national climate wherein the median income of blacks declined to 56 percent of the median income of whites in 1984 (it was 62 percent in 1970), and unemployment in 1985 was 14.9 percent among adult blacks compared to 5.6 percent among adult whites. The unemployment rate in 1985 among black youths—our potential constituency in the college classroom—was 40.1 percent. As the National Urban League's 1986 "State of Black America" report concluded, "economic inequity" between blacks and whites "is greater now than it has been at any time since 1970."

The national economic climate, in short, is a disaster for black people. And, despite notable successes for individual black scholars, the national *academic* climate is a disaster as well. As the numbers and percentages of minority students decrease on our campuses, financial support for area and ethnic studies programs and for related research and scholarship has declined dramatically since the Reagan regime came to power. Ethnic studies programs attract ethnic minorities as faculty members, and ethnic faculty members in turn are able to intervene in the recruitment and retention of ethnic minorities as undergraduate and graduate students and as tenurable faculty members on our college campuses. We must, it seems to me, insist upon the continued and increased funding of ethnic studies programs, allowing these emergent traditions to inform new definitions of the humanities.

As an organization, the MLA must support and seek strategic alliances with other professional academic and social organizations (especially with private foundations) whose interests in these areas overlap with our own desires to "decenter" the profession as we criticize sexism and racism in our scholarly works. Indeed, I believe that it is naïve and irresponsible for us, the members of the MLA, to continue to pretend that we are somehow "above" politics, or that what we think, write, and do can possibly be apolitical. We constitute one of the largest professional organizations in this country. What's more, unlike our counterparts in other branches of the academy, we teach virtually every student who matriculates at the undergraduate level. Even at the most specialized technical institutes in this country, students must study rhetoric and composition. We, as a body, possess an enormous amount of collective authority and power, power which as yet remains unharnessed and untapped, inert and merely potential.

I believe that we, as a body, must begin to take public stands on the social and political issues that plague our society, our campuses, and our profession. Specifically, I believe that we must take public stands on sexism and racism and must sponsor resolutions on specific issues related to affirmative action, at all levels, on our college campuses—from financial aid and minority recruitment of graduate and undergraduate students to the increased recruitment and retention of minority faculty. I believe that we, as a body, must accept, confront, and use our inherent political power for the social good. Why should presidential candidates not include us among the major interest groups they must lobby and court?

I believe that we should extend our membership by offering affiliation status to ethnic academic professional organizations. We should undertake to "decenter" the profession by *actively* expanding our membership base in the Third World, and by seeking funding to enable us to donate copies of our publications, including *PMLA*, to Third World university libraries. As I have said to the Executive Council, I believe that we must allow Third World scholars to pay their membership dues in their own currencies, which they are now unable to do. Because of currency restrictions, inflated national exchange rates, and pitifully low salaries, most of our colleagues at African universities, for example, simply can never afford to join the MLA, let alone purchase our annual bibliographies. We must solicit their membership and involvement in the MLA, if we are ever truly to be a comparative literary association, and not the Modern Language Association of the Western World—the same Western world which the Honorable Mr. Bennett seeks to recover, reify, and enshrine. Let us hope for the day when the annual MLA convention occurs in Abidjan or Nairobi, in Managua or Rio, in Delhi or Jerusalem.

I believe that we should charge the Executive Council to consider the study of literature department curricula—not, as Mr. Bennett would prefer, to return us to the dark ages of "the" canon of the writings of white men, but rather to undertake the ethnic and sexual integration and reformation of ideas concerning the corpus of literature that our respective literature departments teach. Comparative literature will then cease to mean merely Latin, French, Spanish, and German, and will be defined as Yoruba, Swahili, and Zulu as well. It is crucial that we do this, because Mr. Bennett would have us return to those thrilling days of yesteryear, when God was in *His* heaven and all was white with the world, when the only brand of nationalism tolerated in canon formation was white nationalism, and when canon formation was, in fact, the literary version of the "grandfather clause" used in post-Reconstruction America to disenfranchise the newly freed black ex-slaves.

We must engage in this sort of canon deformation precisely because Mr. Bennett is correct: the teaching of literature *is* the teaching of values, the teaching of an aesthetic and political order, in which none of the members of the black community, the minority community, or the women's community were ever able to discover the reflection or representation of their images or to hear the resonances of their cultural voices. The return of "the" canon represents the return of an order in which my people were the subjugated, the voiceless, the invisible, the unrepresented, and the unrepresentable. I, for one, ain't going back there, and I am willing to fight anyone who tries to drag us all back there into that medieval never-never land.

Instead, we must redefine the notion of "the canon" and, indeed, of "the humanities" by including not merely the important writings of white men but the important writings of women and men, whether they be from Africa or Asia, Europe or the Middle East, the First World or the Third. The writings of nonwhite thinkers have long suffered from the tyrannical connection between the words *humanity* and *humanities*. The humanities, as taught in the West since the time of the trivium and the quadrivium, have embodied only Western thought, not the thought of the great cultures of the world. We must encourage an expanded definition of the humanities as the multicultural and multi-linguistic writings of the best that the *world* has had to offer, by integrating the Western tradition with the Asian and African and Arabic traditions. We must see ourselves as the professors of a truly *human* culture, which each day grows ever more vulnerable because nuclear trigger-happy politicians, like Dr. Faust, seem hell-bent upon flirting with the devil.

Let me end by returning to the critique of the subject, to which I alluded earlier. The classic critique of our attempts to reconstitute our own subjectivity as women or as blacks, is that of Derrida: "This is the risk. The effect of Law is to build a structure of the subject, and as soon as you say, 'well, the woman is a subject and this subject deserves equal rights,' and so on—then you are caught in the logic of phallocentrism and you have rebuilt the empire of Law." To expressions such as this, made by a critic whose stands on sexism and racism have been exemplary, we must respond that the Western male subject has been constituted historically for himself and in himself. And, while we readily accept, acknowledge, and partake of the critique of *this* supposedly transcendent subject, to deny us the process of exploring and reclaiming our subjectivity before we critique it, is the critical version of the grandfather clause, the double privileging of categories that happen to be *preconstituted*. Such a position leaves us nowhere, invisible, and voiceless, in the republic of Western letters. In this way, those of us in feminist criticism or African-American criticism who are engaged in the necessary work of canon deformation and reformation confront the skepticism even of those who are allies on other fronts.

Let me be specific. Those of us working in my own tradition confront the hegemony of the Western tradition, generally, and of the larger American tradition, specifically, as we theorize about our tradition and engage in attempts at canon formation. Consider the irony: precisely when we (and other Third World peoples) obtain the complex wherewithal to define our black subjectivity in the republic of Western letters, our theoretical colleagues declare that there is no such thing as a subject; so why should we be bothered with that? Long after white American literature has been anthologized and canonized, and recanonized, our attempts to define a black American canon— foregrounded on its own against a white backdrop—are often decried as racist, separatist, nationalist, or "essentialist" (my favorite term of all). Attempts to derive theories about our literary tradition from this black canon—a canon, I might add, that must include black vernacular forms as well as written literary forms—are often greeted by our colleagues in traditional literature departments as misguided efforts to secede from a union which only recently, and with considerable kicking and screaming, has been forged. What is *wrong* with you people? our friends ask us with genuine passion and concern. After all, aren't we all just citizens of literature?

Well, yes, we must answer. But no. It is clear that every black American text must confess to a complex ancestry, one high and low (literary and vernacular) but also one white and black. There can be no doubt that white texts inform and influence black texts (and vice versa), so that a thoroughly integrated canon of American literature is not only politically sound but *intellectually* sound as well. The attempts of scholars such as Houston Baker, M. H.

Washington, Nellie McKay, and others to define a black American canon, and to derive indigenous literary theories *from* within this canon, are not meant to refute the soundness of these gestures of integration. Rather, it is a question of perspective, of emphasis. Just as we can and must cite a black text within the larger American tradition, we can and must cite it within its own tradition, a tradition not defined by a pseudo-science of racial biology or a mystical shared essence called blackness, but by the repetition and revision of shared themes, topics, and tropes, a process that binds the signal texts of the black tradition into a canon just as surely as separate links bind together into a chain. It is no more, or less, essentialist to make this claim than it is to claim the existence of French, English, German, Russian, or American literature—as long as we proceed inductively, from the texts to the theory, rather than deductively. For nationalism has always been the dwarf in the critical, canonical chess machine. For anyone to deny us the right to engage in attempts to constitute ourselves as discursive subjects is for them to engage in the double privileging of categories that happen to be preconstituted. You cannot, in other words, critique the notion of the subject until a tradition's subjectivity has been firmly established.

We must engage in these activities to resist appropriation of the textual peculiarity of the black tradition by and into the larger American tradition. We must do so, I deeply believe, to step outside of the circle of opposition which notions of a fixed, and transcendent, value-free canon traced around us, even before we had begun to create fictions for and of ourselves. Many of us believe that the time has come for us to valorize our black textual heritage, and to bracket at the margins our white adoptive parentage as we define our own tradition and enshrine its canon—as ironic as we understand this process to be—in institutional, marketable, and teachable forms such as a Norton Anthology. To deny the necessity of this process is to ally ourselves, for whatever reasons and however inadvertently, with the cultural politics of the Right, as exemplified by Mr. Bennett and Mr. Bloom.

Dancing Between Left and Right

Feminism and the Academic Minefield in the 1980s

Annette Kolodny

When, in early 1978, I first began composing an essay on the status of feminist literary criticism within the academy, I saw our situation as precarious but clear. Despite several years of active publication, feminist criticism had secured barely a foothold within English and foreign language departments or mainstream journals. Many who had pioneered the field had been denied tenure, had found temporary haven within a women's studies program, or—like myself—were engaged in Title VII suits. The challenge, therefore, as I understood it a decade ago, was simple. Feminists needed to spell out the theoretical propositions on which our work was grounded in order to open a dialogue with our nonfeminist colleagues; and we needed to hold fast to the political commitments of what we then called the women's liberation movement. "Ideas are important *because* they determine the ways we live, or want to live, in the world," I wrote ten years ago. We dared not, I insisted, confine "those ideas to the study, the classroom, or the pages of our books," separate and separated from the larger world around us (Kolodny 21). To do all this— that is, to open an entirely new field of intellectual inquiry *and* maintain our integrity, while at the same time surviving within institutions that did not want us—seemed to me then tantamount to negotiating a minefield. And, in fact, the essay into which these disparate notes were finally organized was published under the title "Dancing Through the Minefield: Some Observations on the Theory, Practice, and Politics of a Feminist Literary Criticism."

Ten years ago, the image of *dancing* through a minefield was intended to suggest not simply the St. Vitus dance-of-death that too many of us were then experiencing, as promotion and tenure denials detonated around us. The image was also meant to suggest the prospect of a future generation of feminist scholars dancing, without fear, on ground forever deactivated of its explosive anxieties—anxieties that I labeled in the original essay as "the male fear of sharing power and significance with women" (Kolodny 22).

Now, ten years later, despite the continuing reluctance of the courts to act favorably on academic sex discrimination suits; despite changing demographics in the 1970s which shrank the college-age population and, with it, the academic job market; and despite repeated Reagan cutbacks in aid to education throughout the 1980s, which also took their toll on job opportunities, feminist scholars and feminist inquiry seem nonetheless to have attained some measure of security on the academic landscape. The Summer 1987 *MLA Newsletter* noted that "among contemporary approaches to literary study, feminist criticism had had the greatest impact on curriculum." Citing a 1986 survey of English doctoral programs, the *Newsletter* reported that "87% of the departments surveyed ranked [feminist criticism] as important" ("Survey" 12). In the popular media, the *New York Times* Sunday magazine of December 6, 1987, announced that "feminist criticism, once a sort of illicit half sister in the academic world, has assumed a respectable place in the family order." Peter Brooks, Professor of French and Comparative Literature at Yale, is quoted in that same article as declaring, "Anyone worth his salt in literary criticism today has to become something of a feminist" (Kolbert 110).

Clearly, feminism in the academy has succeeded in opening a vigorous and ongoing dialogue with literary critics and scholars of all stripes and schools. The question to be asked now is: What kind of dialogue has it been?

According to statistics from the National Research Council, women began to earn the majority of English and foreign language doctorates in 1980, and by 1986 women represented 59% of the Ph.D.'s in these fields. Figures from the Modern Language Association "indicate that in tenure-track appointments in literature departments, women are roughly on a par with men" (Kolbert 112). To be sure, women remain clustered disproportionately in two- and four-year institutions, rather than research universities, and at the lower end of both the rank and salary scales. Even so, the fact remains that during the 1980s, women became numerically significant within literature departments, and many among these were women doing feminist work.

As literary studies became progressively more feminized, however, the centers of professional prestige shifted from departments to summer schools and institutes of critical theory. Staffed largely by white males from elite institutions, these new alignments of power included in their early years a variety of post-structuralist theorists with practitioners of deconstruction eventually predominating. In recent years, the deconstructionists have been joined by some Marxists. If the pairing seems an odd one—the deconstructionists inherently uncertain about any political agenda and the Marxists presumably committed to one—what must be understood is that yoking these men together was neither shared ideology nor shared practice but, instead, the appeal of establishing boundaries. The Marxist impulse to preserve the referential text for the purpose of asserting social and historical contexts for literary study might stand side by side with deconstruction's resistance to anything other than text *because* high-powered men were bent on fleeing not only an increasingly feminized professoriat but, as well, an increasingly persuasive feminist practice rooted in literary history and the retrieval of lost traditions. In other words, the male "muscle" of the profession aimed at theory *in order to* distinguish itself from a feminism that had never been systematically theory-driven.

The ironies were everywhere. By sharing the stage with the Marxists, deconstructionists who elsewhere challenged the notion of reality in favor of a tissue of conventions of indeterminate meanings inadvertently gave new legitimacy to a *praxis* derived from materialist determinism. At the same time, a new breed of Marxists found itself in the peculiar position of rejecting the historicizing and contextualizing practices of feminism while adopting some of the language and postures of deconstruction, thereby effectively blunting its ability to maintain a critical discourse with real-world political engagements.

If feminist literary criticism in the United States had never been theory-driven, it also had never been shy of entering the theoretical arena. Indeed, by the end of the 1970s, Peggy Kamuf, Jane Gallop, and others were already taking advantage of the ferment in French psychoanalytic and philosophical circles to playfully, even teasingly (in Gallop's work especially), rival the men in the manipulation of arcane vocabularies and imported theoretical paradigms. In 1980, Deborah McDowell responded to an earlier piece by Barbara Smith in the attempt to formulate a theoretical base for black feminist criticism. And in 1981 Elaine Showalter offered *gynocriticism* as both method and theory. By 1986 the sometimes heated debates among feminist critics in the American academy over the political implications of theoretical models drawn from Lacan and Derrida resulted in Elizabeth Meese's plea for a polyvocal dialogue between Anglo-American and French critical schools in *Crossing the Double-Cross: The Practice of Feminist Criticism*. And in 1987, in *Revolution and the Word,* Cathy Davidson demonstrated the value of attending to all these crosscurrents by gracefully employing both Foucault and Derrida for a startling new analysis of the rise of the novel in eighteenth-century America.

On the one hand, what has not yet emerged from this intense feminist foray into theory is any kind of synthesis. Feminist theorists in general and Anglo-American feminist literary scholars in particular continue to contest the wisdom of grafting feminist inquiry onto the masculinist roots of Freud,

Lacan, or even Derrida (whose theoretical positions on race and gender have often been acknowledged as exemplary). The resistance to grounding feminism solely in deconstructive readings, moreover—despite deconstruction's signal usefulness in unraveling any text's hidden gender assumptions—is bound to solidify with the revelation that its major American exponent published collaborationist and anti-Semitic essays in 1940s Belgium. Deconstruction's disavowal of politics and history, its refusal of closure or judgment, many feminists surmise, may well also have represented the late Paul de Man's strategy for escaping both judgment and history.[1] In any event, by refusing any one overarching theory or theoretical paradigm, feminist literary criticism in the United States has sustained the widest possible variety of practices, remaining polyvocal, multitheoretical, and impossible to simplify or contain.

On the other hand, what may have emerged as a result of feminism's proven proficiency in theoretical discourse is a new move "against theory." Stanley Fish's is hardly the only voice to declare "theory's day is dying," when pages of journals like *Critical Inquiry* give rise to more and more collections like *Against Theory: Literary Studies and the New Pragmatism*. After all, as Cary Nelson has suggested, with feminism shifting "the attention of theory . . . from how to interpret literature to how the discipline of literary studies is constituted," theory no longer stands as a secure bastion of privilege. With feminists doing the theorizing, Nelson astutely observes, the pressures on the profession are a good deal "more threatening" ("Against English" 48).

Even more problematic, however, is that feminist theorizing has emerged as a new *cachet*. Male critics rush to prove that they are at least "something of a feminist." Within some departments, feminist critical theory is *the* hot new field that graduate students ignore at their peril. And feminist theorists are now regularly invited to join the faculties of the summer schools and institutes that once excluded us. What is so sobering in all this is that the originating revolutionary potential of feminism is slowly being eroded. The male critics who would "profess" feminism too often read only the same selective sampling, thus establishing for themselves their own feminist "canon" and evading feminism's hard-won diversity of voices. The feminist invited to a summer school or institute of critical theory is invariably a token, her particular style of theorizing forced to stand synecdochically for a whole it cannot possibly represent. And, at the graduate level especially, severing of the link between feminist literary inquiry and feminism as a political agenda has intensified as the seminar in feminist theory becomes solely a means to professional advancement. As one European visitor—upon assigning a selection of readings from Irigaray and Kristeva—told her graduate students at a prestigious eastern university, "None of this has anything to do with the real world." She was not interested, she explained, in the "empirical." For some in the class, it was precisely the assurance they were hoping for.

All of this returns me to the question I posed at the outset: What kind of dialogue has it been?

In a paper originally delivered to the Alternative English Faculty at Cambridge (and subsequently incorporated into his *Walter Benjamin: or Towards a Revolutionary Criticism*), Terry Eagleton concluded his consideration of Marxist aesthetics by turning to "feminist criticism" as "a paradigm" for a potentially " 'revolutionary literary criticism.' " Feminist criticism had not yet achieved that potential, Eagleton explained, because it "is still notably underdeveloped, and much of it so far has been empiricist, unsubtle and theoretically thin" (99–100). Because Eagleton made these observations at the end of the 1970s and prior to feminism's subsequent intensive engagement with theory, his remarks may seem innocent enough, if a bit peevish. After all, with a publication record less than a decade old, by the close of the seventies the new feminism was already nothing less than revolutionary in its impact (which is why Eagleton had to take it into account). But because they were spoken almost a decade ago, Eagleton's words are easy to dismiss either as impatience or as a profound misunderstanding of Anglo-American feminism's continuing commitment to the empirical *as part of* its theoretical base. When remarks like this are made even today, by contrast, they suggest not only the power of the fantasy projections of those who wish feminism had remained "underdeveloped." They suggest also the condescending—if unspoken—judgment that feminists still haven't "got it right" and that our enterprise would be much better off in male hands. As a result, in the dialogue that has unfolded in the eighties, one hears recognizable echoes of Eagleton's early remarks as one male critic after another either chides the feminist for not doing things *his* way or for not meeting *his* expectations of what she should be about.

These complaints take many forms, of course, and are rarely articulated so boldly. A special issue of *New Literary History* on "Feminist Directions" is instructive here because it includes, among other items, a group of invited comments on Ellen Messer-Davidow's essay, "The Philosophical Bases of Feminist Literary Criticisms," along with Messer-Davidow's response. The Autumn 1987 issue thus affords a unique opportunity both to catch the dialogue in progress and, with that, to compare the strategies of three quite different male critics when engaging feminist theory. My concern, let me emphasize, is not with the overt arguments for and against Messer-Davidow's position but, rather, with the covert meanings of the locutions through which the arguments are expressed.

Cary Nelson, for example, welcomes Messer-Davidow's essay not as an original contribution to theory but as "one of a number of overviews and syntheses of feminist scholarship that have appeared in recent years" ("Feminism, Language, and Philosophy," 117). "There is a real need" for such syntheses, Nelson continues, "first, [because] they help maintain a significant basis for partial consensus within feminism" and "second [because] there is a special need for latecomers to feminism, most often men, to encounter general overviews that will help prevent them from wholly misconstruing feminism's central aims" (118). While Nelson's views are generously enough offered, they nonetheless place "latecomers to feminism, most often men," in a special relationship to feminist inquiry that nowhere replicates the demands upon women who enter male-dominated domains of knowledge. That is, the male latecomer is tacitly disburdened of the need to honor the corpus of work by encountering it in the original. In this instance, syntheses and general overviews will suffice. That general overviews are by necessity reductive, Nelson altogether ignores. And this fact suggests that the call for periodic remappings of the field may disguise a more sinister agenda: containment.

The issue is complicated by the numbers of males who seem increasingly eager to offer the overviews.[2] For example, when Eugene Goodheart (who is not sympathetic to feminism) wants to make his case against the epistemological bases of feminist criticisms as put forth by Messer-Davidow, he invokes the authority of a male feminist critic Jonathan Culler (who presumably *is* sympathetic to feminism). The irony is that Goodheart can effectively construct an argument against Messer-Davidow *because* "Jonathan Culler provides a model for feminist criticism of an instructively problematic kind" (181). If this sort of thing continues, feminist literary criticism is in danger of becoming yet another discourse in which men speak to men about women.[3]

In this context, *how* we are spoken about becomes crucial. Consider Gerald Graff's response to Messer-Davidow in that same Autumn 1987 *New Literary History*. Graff denies the originality of Messer-Davidow's epistemological system by assuming it under more familiar—and nonfeminist—categories. "The dispositions Messer-Davidow classifies as feminist . . . are generally reminiscent of the world view which has been called 'contextualism' . . . or 'historicism,' and is exemplified in such tendencies as modern pragmatism, existentialism, and post-structuralism. In short," concludes Graff, "what Messer-Davidow puts forth as a uniquely feminist basis is a critique of positivist functional rationality that had been developed by innumerable philosophers and poets long before feminism became a cultural force" (137–38). What gives the game away is that Graff's list of feminist features—supposedly derived from Messer-Davidow's article—includes items like " 'interactive,' participatory" and "sees texts as part of a contextual field" (137) but altogether omits Messer-Davidow's central point that feminist inquiry is an epistemological investigation into how we come to hold the ideas we do and, more specifically, an inquiry into the epistemology "of ideas about sex and gender that people express in literary and critical media" (Messer-Davidow 77). But "ideas about sex and gender" nowhere appear on Graff's list. In consequence, by attempting to assume Messer-Davidow under "a critique of positivist functional rationality," Graff must also distort what Messer-Davidow and feminism are about.

When Dale Spender published *Women of Ideas and What Men Have Done to Them* in 1982 and Joanna Russ published her wickedly amusing *How to Suppress Women's Writing* a year later, both codified the ways in which, historically, women's ideas and women's writings had been routinely suppressed, misattributed, misrepresented, and appropriated. If the quantity and quality of two solid decades of feminist scholarship have insured that suppression and misattribution seem no longer possible, Graff's strategies demonstrate that appropriation and misrepresentation certainly are.

Granted, all this may *look like* a dialogue. But one has to question how fair or how fruitful the exchange when one side so often favors boundary-making, containment, appropriation, and misrepresentation. The point I am making is that our tenacity and perseverance have led us not only toward hard-won success but, as well, onto yet another minefield. For, the anxieties that laid the minefield in the 1970s are still with us in the eighties: "the male fear of sharing power and significance with women." Ten years ago, I recommended opening a dialogue with our nonfeminist colleagues as a means to dismantling the minefield. As the eighties come to a close, it seems to me that the dialogue is in process and, for the foreseeable future, inevitable. For the nineties, however, renewing our dialogue with one another may prove the necessary strategy for dismantling these newest versions of the minefield.

Those of us who came to feminist literary criticism out of the 1960s New Left and the consciousness-raising groups of the late sixties and early seventies must find ways of reaching out to the Ph.D. candidates of the 1980s and 1990s for whom feminism will otherwise become merely another entree into sophisticated critical theory circles. We must remind these young women and men that feminism is a visionary politics which declares that a theory is only as good as its practice. To become theoretically sophisticated about how gender and racial hierarchies structure both knowledge and cultural institutions imposes upon us the responsibility to act in the world to dismantle institutionalized inequities. If respectability is achieved at the cost of this visionary politics, then feminist inquiry is rendered an empty, enervated exercise, essentially timid and accommodationist.[4] The challenge implied by feminist inquiry in any discipline, after all, is not whether you can *do* it but whether you can *live* it.

At the same time, those of us for whom feminism was a healing, galvanizing force because it revealed the hidden contradictions in our lives must extend a hand to a younger generation for whom feminism loomed as threatening and hurtful. These are the children of mothers who, emboldened by feminism's call to liberation and independence, tried to reject traditional family roles in a society that offered their offspring no compensating structures and amid a movement too new to prepare us all for the consequences of such radical change. As one young woman told me recently, "I was twelve years old when my mother discovered feminism. She kept talking about finding herself, and so she went back to school and ended up a lawyer. But she wasn't my mother anymore. During the years when I needed her most, I felt she just wasn't there for me. And neither was anyone else." Only now, as a beginning graduate student timidly auditing her first women's studies course, is this young woman beginning to develop any historical understanding of the hard choices made by her mother. And only now, in consequence, can she begin to confront her longtime hostility to feminism and contemplate retrieving a relationship that for years has been mired in bitterness and mutual recrimination. For sons and daughters such as these, at the very least, explanations are due.

We must also begin a conversation about our fears of cooption. Colleagues who are sympathetic to feminism and know that they have benefitted from its efforts cannot keep refusing the label "feminist" because they are fearful of cooption by some monolithic dogma. These friends must be disabused of the notion that feminism enjoins any kind of political litmus test. By the same token, those of us who openly name ourselves feminist must together rethink our habitual aversion to entering the power structure(s). If we are to protect the gains of the last decade and—as we claim—change the structures of power, then we must accept the responsibility to position ourselves in such a way as to make change possible. Within academe, that means branching out from our prior administrative posts as directors of women's studies programs and women's research centers to become department chairs, deans, provosts, and even university presidents—in substantial numbers and not merely as the occasional token.

This is not to say that we dare abandon the forces for change that exist outside of established institutional structures. On the contrary, real change can occur only when there are pressure groups without and responsive power brokers within. Though individually each of us can be at only one place at one time, together we must be everywhere.

If in the 1980s, a coterie of relatively secure feminists increasingly made its appearance in the classroom and faculty club with manicured nails, silk blouses, and designer suits, then in the nineties that same group of feminists must once again risk dirt under our nails because we shared a tent in an anti-apartheid shantytown erected with our students; or brave purple smears on our hands and cheeks because we'd been running mimeo machines to help underpaid support staff organize a union; or forego the silk blouses altogether because we're financing a local shelter for battered women and children. Feminists who have "made it" professionally, in other words, must keep open the lines of communication and support with those still in struggle, recognizing that *our* gains have not benefitted all. Legislation to assure unpaid child-care leaves may be welcome at the upper end of the income brackets, for example, but such legislation hardly helps the mother for whom a week without pay means a week without food. To renew our dialogue with different constituencies of women, both on campus and off, not only underscores in activist terms our theoretical commitment to diversity. It also underscores the ancient truism that we are as much the teachers of our students by what we do outside the classroom as by what we do inside.

Perhaps the most important dialogue that we need to initiate, though, is the one about ourselves and our history. The writing of history, for the most part, has been an institutional practice, invented first to justify the state and later adapted by a variety of elites to promulgate the divine mandate for established authorities or the natural inevitability of existing power arrangements. The official history of the academy is no different, derived as it is from selected records and disseminated through campus publications like newsletters and alumni magazines. What feminists know about the academy has no place in this telling; and when feminism is incorporated, it is most likely to emerge as something like the celebration of a "Post-feminist Yale," the cover story of the Summer 1987 *Yale Alumni Magazine.* But behind these authorized versions is another story: a story commencing with the first women who dared introduce feminism to the classroom or organized on behalf of credited women's studies programs, a history often expunged from the record and from memory just as surely as those women were expunged from the tenure rolls. Likewise, those few of us who survived the early years need to tell our own stories: stories about the exhilaration of organizing around women's studies programs and the camaraderie of establishing campus women's centers; stories about moving like nomads from campus to campus in the revolving door that represented academic employment for feminists throughout the 1970s; and stories about tenure denials and lawsuits. Those of us who survived and even achieved some measure of prominence must also begin to talk frankly about frustration and burnout.

Those who came after us must tell us what it has been like for them, candidly assessing both the legacy and the burdens that an older generation may have unwittingly imposed. We need to hear from that younger generation of feminists who chose to teach in community colleges and to organize within working-class neighborhoods, just as we need to learn from those new Ph.D.'s ambivalent about feminism even as they acknowledge its boost to their careers or its influence upon their scholarship.

The practice of feminist literary criticism is the most demanding practice I know. It has never simply been about decoding the gender and racial biases in literary history or deconstructing the gender, race, and class assumptions in literature and criticism, nor even about recuperating individual women writers and entire female traditions. Within the academy, it is and always has been a moral and ethical stance that seeks to change the structures of knowledge and, with that, the institutional structures in which knowledge gets made and codified.

That is a tall order, and those who have been about it for the last twenty years are very tired. At times, we look in vain for a politicized younger generation to carry on our work, even as we work tirelessly to see that the younger generations of feminist academics are hired and tenured and paid fairly. It pains us to see feminism used opportunistically by those who never experienced its urgencies.

Even so, my appeal that we begin a multi- and intergenerational dialogue about ourselves and our histories must not be misconstrued as a call for senior women to tell their juniors how to do things or what to do. In the changed circumstances of the nineties, new challenges will demand the invention of new strategies. The examples from the past are to serve neither as models nor as guidelines but rather as guideposts to the continued possibility of future change.

This same dialogue, I hope, will also generate at least three strategies for dismantling the minefield laid in the eighties. First and foremost, it will remind us—as Arlyn Diamond has put it—that "the feminist search for an authentic intellectual voice is a collective task, which expands as we work at it, and gets more exciting as it expands and as we share it" (206). Secondly, if we begin to take responsibility for recovering our history, we may blunt the efforts of those eager to write our history for us, determining which of us shall be read and cited, and proclaiming us a historical curiosity in this supposedly postfeminist era. Finally, by recovering the full diversity of our history as we lived it—and not as some cursory overview homogenized it—we may at the same time recover our original energizing politics. We will remember anew the intimate link between intellectual inquiry and the consequences of that inquiry for how we act in the world. And we will proclaim again that theory devoid of activist politics isn't feminism but, rather, pedantry and moral abdication.

Notes

Conversations with Elissa Gelfand, Carolyn Heilbrun, Carolyn Karcher, Susan Koppelman, Ellen Messer-Davidow, Alicia Ostriker, Amy Thomas, Jane Tompkins, and Emily Toth helped me focus some of the issues raised in these pages. The good ideas are theirs, the murky sections all mine.

1 See Wiener.
2 See, for example, Ruthven.
3 This has perhaps already happened in the field of men's studies. Once a direct offshoot of and parallel to feminist inquiry—but practiced by men with an emphasis on the social construction of male gender roles—men's studies has managed to achieve a wholly new misogyny. In "Margaret Mead, Men's Studies, and Feminist Scholarship," an address to the 1987 meeting of the American Studies Association, historian Lois Banner noted that recent scholarship in men's studies tended to ignore the work of feminists, even on the same topic. "In print, I notice no women associated with men's studies; articles by very few women are included in their new anthologies," said Banner. "This is too much a movement of men speaking to men" (4). In effect, as Banner made clear, these latest moves of men's studies seem intent on reinstating male authority on the subject of gender and intent, as well, on editing women out of a discourse that we were responsible for initiating.
4 White makes a similar observation about "Marxist thought," p. 143.

Bibliography

Banner, Lois W. "Margaret Mead, Men's Studies, and Feminist Scholarship." *American Studies Association Newsletter* 11.1 (March 1988): 2–6.

Culler, Jonathan. *On Deconstruction: Theory and Criticism after Structuralism.* Ithaca: Cornell University Press, 1982.

Davidson, Cathy N. *Revolution and the Word: The Rise of the Novel in America.* New York: Oxford University Press, 1987.

Diamond, Arlyn. "Interdisciplinary Studies and a Feminist Community." *For Alma Mater: Theory and Practice in Feminist Scholarship.* Ed. Paula A. Treichler, Cheris Kramarae, and Beth Stafford. Urbana: University of Illinois Press, 1985. 199–226.

Eagleton, Terry. *Walter Benjamin: or Towards a Revolutionary Criticism.* London: New Left Books, 1981.

Elder, Sharon. "Next Steps for Superwomen." *Yale Alumni Magazine* 50.8 (Summer 1987): 28–33.

Fish, Stanley. "Consequences." *Against Theory: Literary Studies and the New Pragmatism.* Ed. W. J. T. Mitchell. Chicago: University of Chicago Press, 1985. 106–31.

Gallop, Jane. "The Ghost of Lacan, the Trace of Language." *Diacritics* 5.4 (Winter 1975): 18–24.

Goodheart, Eugene. "Against Coercion." *New Literary History* 19 (Autumn 1987): 179–85.

Graff, Gerald. "Response to 'The Philosophical Bases of Feminist Literary Criticisms.'" *New Literary History* 19 (Autumn 1987): 135–38.

Kamuf, Peggy. "Abraham's Wake." *Diacritics* (March 1979): 32–43.

Kolbert, Elizabeth. "Literary Feminism Comes of Age." *New York Times Magazine* 6 December 1987: 110–17.

Kolodny, Annette. "Dancing Through the Minefield: Some Observations on the Theory, Practice, and Politics of a Feminist Literary Criticism." *Feminist Studies* 6 (1980): 1–25.

McDowell, Deborah E. "New Directions for Black Feminist Criticism." 1980. Rpt. *The New Feminist Criticism: Essays on Women, Literature, and Theory.* Ed. Elaine Showalter. New York: Pantheon, 1985. 186–99.

Meese, Elizabeth A. *Crossing the Double-Cross: The Practice of Feminist Criticism.* Chapel Hill: University of North Carolina Press, 1986.

Messer-Davidow, Ellen. "The Philosophical Bases of Feminist Literary Criticisms." *New Literary History* 19 (Autumn 1987): 63–103.

Nelson, Cary. "Against English: Theory and the Limits of the Discipline." *Profession* 87 (Modern Language Association): 46–52.

———. "Feminism, Language, and Philosophy." *New Literary History* 19 (Autumn 1987): 117–28.

Russ, Joanna. *How to Suppress Women's Writing.* Austin: University of Texas Press, 1983.

Ruthven, K. K. *Feminist Literary Studies: An Introduction.* Cambridge: Cambridge University Press, 1984.

Showalter, Elaine. "Feminist Criticism in the Wilderness." 1981. Rpt. *The New Feminist Criticism: Essays on Women, Literature, and Theory.* Ed. Showalter. New York: Pantheon, 1985. 243–70.

Smith, Barbara. "Toward a Black Feminist Criticism." 1977. Rpt. *The New Feminist Criticism: Essays on Women, Literature, and Theory.* Ed. Elaine Showalter. New York: Pantheon, 1985. 168–85.

Spender, Dale. *Women of Ideas and What Men Have Done to Them.* London: Routledge & Kegan Paul, 1982.

"Survey of Doctoral Programs in English." *MLA Newsletter* (Summer 1987): 12.

White, Hayden. *The Content of the Form: Narrative Discourse and Historical Representation.* Baltimore: Johns Hopkins University Press, 1987.

Wiener, Jon. "Deconstructing de Man." *The Nation* 9 January 1988: 22–24.

Language Politics in the U.S.A.

The English-Only Movement

Ana Celia Zentella

There is no doubt that the proponents of the amendment to make English the official language of the United States have hit upon a pulsating raw nerve of dissatisfaction and fear in the American psyche. As the century draws to a close, Americans are looking around and not liking what they see. Home doesn't feel like home anymore. There are too many different people, with different races and faces, different foods and music, different ideas and ways of doing things; and too many don't speak English.

Ah, but THIS problem has an easy solution. The painless antidote promising quick relief—a law that declares "English shall be the official language of the United States"—in that wonderful tamper-proof package, the Constitution, has captured the American market and is selling like the proverbial hotcakes. In scholarly books and journals as well as in newspaper editorials and popular magazines, on radio and television talk shows, in professional conferences and labor union halls, in checkout lines and bowling lanes, and all across bipartisan lines, the English-only panacea has been swallowed up eagerly across the country. During 1987 alone, thirty-seven states considered amendments to their constitutions that would declare English the official language; in thirteen states it is official, and in 1988 Florida, Texas, Arizona, and Colorado will have the question on the ballot. With one single, disarmingly simple and deceptive piece of legislation, the advocates of English-only propose that what they view as a major problem in today's United States—the 4 percent of the population who do not speak English—can be solved. Here is finally the chance to do something, to make a difference as an individual, together with others who share the same concerns, the same discomfort. It is no wonder that U.S. English and English First, the two leading organizations sponsoring the amendment, can depend on the financial contributions of over one-half million members. I can picture contributors writing out their checks: some righteously racist, but others—the majority?—experiencing the same good feeling I get when I contribute to the St. Labre Indian School, but with that extra dose of warm pride that comes from being wrapped in the American flag. This has been turned into a patriotic cause. In its publications U.S. English ("Fact Sheet" 1) claims that "a common language is necessary to preserve the basic internal unity required for political stability and national cohesion." English First, "a project of the Committee to Protect the Family," promises that "this amendment will stop a direct attack on our American way of life" (Horn 1). Both organizations appeal to the most noble patriotic sentiments. As a result, anyone who questions the need for this legislation or the motivations behind it runs the risk of having her/his patriotism impugned. It is as unacceptable as challenging motherhood and apple pie. "How can you be against the English language?" "Don't you support national unity?" One leading advocate, Rusty Butler, who was hired by former Secretary of Education Bennett, fans the flames of suspicion by claiming that "the language situation in the U.S. could feed and guide terrorism." He goes so far as to claim that bilingual education has "serious implications for national security" (10).

Given this atmosphere, how can I respond? To the righteous racists, there is probably nothing I could say that would convince them. But what about the uncommitted stranger on the plane who asks, "What do you think of this amendment?"; and what about the honest supporters of English only? What can I say to those who feel like strangers in their own country because of bilingual signs or ballots, and who earnestly believe ex-Senator Hayakawa, the linguist, founder, and honorary chair of U.S. English, when he claims that the "magical bond of a common language" ("Why" 16) can "gradually overcome differences of religion and race" ("Questions" 1). Will this ideal really be achieved by requiring that English alone be used in every government-supported endeavor? On the basis of my experiences as the daughter of immigrants, as a Spanish-English bilingual, as a feminist, and as a linguist, I have to say that the English-only amendment will NOT realize these goals, nor will it teach English. Instead, it will have injurious repercussions, particularly for Hispanic women, for the teaching of foreign languages, for the education of immigrant children, for medical and legal services, for voting rights and, consequently, for democracy. Additionally, by preying on what perhaps are natural fears of difference, this movement plays into the hands of ethnocentrists and racists and fosters divisiveness, not unity. Sadly, it offers a simplistic solution to a complex issue and does not address the fundamental problems; Fishman has labeled it aptly the "classical wrong solution to the wrong problem" (" 'English Only' " 15).

What leads me to paint such a negative picture of an effort that seems so well intentioned? My Mexican father and Puerto Rican mother are the most immediate and compelling reasons I have for worrying about the repercussions of an English language amendment (hereafter ELA). My father, a mailman with an elementary school education and the founder of New York's Centro Mexicano, a cultural organization, was devoted equally to Spanish and English and welcomed contact with other languages and cultures as well. The vision of the U.S. that he fought to defend in World War II was one that recognized the primacy of English as a lingua franca, but not at the expense of forbidding the use of other languages to provide crucial services, or by fostering disrespect for those who required them. He died recently and would have been affected by the amendment, but not so seriously as my seventy-nine-year-old mother, who lives alone. This is particularly ironic because, as a Puerto Rican, she already has suffered the consequences of an English-only movement. "Mami" cries whenever she sings "The Star-Spangled Banner," but she does not know the Puerto Rican anthem because it was not taught in that U.S. colony when she was growing up. That was one repercussion of the policy that the U.S. imposed in Puerto Rico from 1898 to 1950, which required that the entire legal and educational system function in English; another was an over 80 percent dropout rate in the schools. As a result, there was a great deal of social upheaval and political unrest in the island, forcing a change in the policy (Zentella, "Language Variety"). One goal that the English-only policy in Puerto Rico did NOT achieve was widespread English proficiency. Now, the same type of policy that denied my mother an adequate education in her childhood is threatening to make her old age more trying. Although she can converse with anyone and read newspapers in English, she still needs federally funded bilingual services and documents for help with complicated medical, Social Security, and veterans' benefits. Availability of these services could have made the difference between dependence and independence in the final years of my parents' lives.

Women and Children Most Seriously Affected

In general women are more likely than men to be affected by an English-only policy, because the scarcity of child-care facilities and of job training programs keeps women at home and does not provide them with significant opportunities to learn English. Women in language-minority communities endure greater unemployment and poverty than men, and mothers of preschoolers are the most seriously affected. Their encounters with the bureaucracies that must be contacted in order to protect their children's education and welfare are usually painful and frequently degrading, particularly when their lack of English is misinterpreted as lack of competence. Since women speak English less than men, yet many have the sole responsibility for heading the household, the English-only amendment—which would eliminate the provision of federally supported information and services in languages other than English—is primarily an anti-female, anti-child, as well as anti-elderly amendment.[1] It would be a sad commentary on the closing decade of the twentieth century, one that added insult to injury, if, after having denied women legal protection for equal rights, the U.S. Constitution were amended to deny millions of people, most of them women, essential human services because of linguistic differences.

No one seriously committed to the equality of women can support the English-only amendment. Significant comparisons between the threats posed by the ELA and the concerns of the feminist movement emerge as obvious when we consider the damaging repercussions of the proposed legislation and the impact of living in a sexist, male-dominated society. Feminist scholarship in an ever-increasing number of areas has documented the ways in which males control most aspects of human life, thereby perpetuating and justifying continued male dominance, but feminist analyses of linguistics are the most appropriate for this discussion.[2]

A gender perspective in language research reveals that the vocabulary and structure of a language, as well as its patterns of interaction, reflect and help perpetuate the subordinate role of women in society. Even the prevailing approach to the study of language itself reflects this reality: it follows a dichotomous model that polarizes integral parts of a whole and subsumes one to another, the way women are differentiated from men and subordinated to them (Gershuny). Thus, modern linguistic theory divorces competence from performance, theory from behavior, and form from function, favoring the first element in each of the pairs as superior to the other. The insistence of English-only supporters on a nation unified by only one language, disregarding a multicultural past, present, and future, has its parallel in the decontextualized approach to the study of Chomsky's "ideal speaker" which leaves out class and gender differences and the sociopolitical rules that guide each interaction. And just as the English language subsumes female under male in the use of such gender nominals as *mankind* and the gender-marking pronouns *he/his* for women, the English-only amendment, also in the name of greater ease in communication, seeks to formalize and perpetuate the inferior status of languages other than English. The idea of a monolingual English speaker conveys a strength denied the monolingual Spanish speaker; bilingualism in Anglos is viewed as enriching, whereas bilingualism in language minorities is often characterized as a handicap, cognitively confusing. Similarly, a positive semantic load is given to male terms such as *master* and *bachelor,* in contrast to *mistress* and *spinster;* similarly, *aggressive males* are evaluated more favorably than *aggressive females.*

Yet another parallel can be drawn between the arguments of ELA proponents, who maintain that abandonment of the mother tongue and proficiency in English are the keys to economic success, and those who encourage women to replace a polite, expressive style with the competitive, controlling style of male speech if they hope to get their share of power and respect. But women who adopt male styles of speech find that they may be labeled unfeminine, or even castrating, and are still denied equal status; in the same way, minorities who know English well, including many black Americans, native Americans, and the children of immigrants, remain among the poorest in this country. Both approaches devalue speakers of the nondominant groups, even when they acquire the dominant ways of speaking, and both trivialize racism and sexism, ignoring the fundamental sociopolitical realities which perpetuate these inequalities.

The detractors of linguistic and cultural pluralism and the detractors of feminism share a "hydraulic" (Hakuta)—fittingly male—view of genders and languages; there is room for only one, and any talk of coexistence or sharing is interpreted as replacement of the present dominator with its subordinate. The fear is that Spanish will rule/overpower English and that women will rule/overpower men. The detractors also share the same narrow vision of the United States in the twenty-first century, one that reasserts and legally buttresses a slightly modified definition of the old WASP power elite. It is WASPMEM—white, Anglo-Saxon, Protestant, middle-class, English-speaking, and male.

The Anti-Spanish Movement

A desire to replace that repressive view of the future with one that promises greater liberation, a desire prompted by the experiences of my elderly parents and the desperate situation of the members of my community, particularly the women, is enough to make me a fervent opponent of the English language amendment. In addition, as a Spanish-English bilingual, and as a linguist interested in the future of language study in the United States, I see other damaging repercussions of the English-only movement; Hispanics are experiencing some of them already. Although all thirty-five million speakers of other languages in this country are likely to suffer the consequences, there is no doubt that the English-only movement is primarily an anti-Spanish movement. Singling out any language group for attack is indefensible, but it is particularly saddening when the language under attack has coexisted with English in the United States from the beginning. The Spanish settlement in St. Augustine in 1565 predated the arrival of the English-speaking colonists in Roanoke, Jamestown, and Plymouth. Spanish was flourishing in seven states, four of them in the Southeast, by the middle of the seventeenth century, when there were English settlements in only six states (Beardsley). Today, Spanish is spoken by approximately twenty million people across the entire country.

The supporters of U.S. English seem unaware of the prominent role that Spanish has played throughout U.S. history. This is obvious in statements that lament "a few cities in which Spanish is the dominant language" and "entire regions of the U.S. in which Spanish is ALREADY a viable language" ("Frequently Used Arguments" 8) [emphasis added]. Other distortions of history appear in their literature, for example, the claim that "for the first time, a majority of migrants speak just one language—Spanish" (8). This simply is not true: in 1790 German speakers composed 8.7 percent of the U.S. population, compared to 7.9 percent for Hispanics today (Crawford, "Optimal Policies"). The number of Germans continued to increase in the nineteenth century; between 1830 and 1890, five million Germans settled in the United States. Those who discredit current bilingual education programs as a Hispanic pork-barrel should know that, in an effort to encourage German support for the new public school system, some public schools in Wisconsin and the rural areas of the Midwest were run entirely in German during that period (Perlmann). During World War I, however, it became a crime in many states to teach in German or to speak German on the street, on the telephone, or in church; there were even public burnings of German books. Some eighteen thousand people were charged under these repressive laws by 1921 (Crawford, "Optimal Policies"). In 1923, the Supreme Court ultimately struck down statutes in over twenty states which made English the official language and prohibited the teaching of other languages in the classroom. That landmark decision, *Meier* v. *Nebraska,* proclaimed that the "protection of the constitution extends to all, to those who speak other languages as well as to those born with English on the tongue" (cited in Combs and Trasvina 24). It is precisely this protection of the Constitution that the English-only movement intends to rob us of today. Their English language amendment would be the first addition to the Constitution that denies any rights to U.S. citizens since the prohibition legislation, and the only one since that legislation was repealed.

The Lessons of U.S. Language History

The German experience in the early decades of this century and the Spanish experience in recent decades exemplify two facts that emerge from the work of historians of language policy in the United States (Heath, Fishman, Macías). One is the inevitable link that exists between the treatment of speakers of other languages in our midst and the extent of foreign language competence in the country. The other regards the level of language tolerance as a response to macro-level national and economic pressures. The isolationism of the first half of this century which led to linguistic xenophobia had a devastating effect on the study of foreign languages in the United States. Some languages, such as German, have never recovered fully. Between 1915 and 1932, the number of students of German declined by 98 percent. Other languages also suffered: 83 percent of all high school students in 1910 studied foreign languages, but only 22 percent in 1948 (Simon). The country was linguistically unprepared for World War II, when the need for speakers of other languages became an issue of military security. Today, when fewer than 18 percent of U.S. high school students take language courses and 53 percent of our colleges allow students to graduate without studying any language other than English, businessmen claim that our linguistic incompetence is partly responsible for our inability to meet the economic challenges of the next century. At least three national commissions have decried U.S. monolingualism, calling for its cure, yet nurturing the ability of thirty-five million Americans who speak other languages is not a priority in the development of the nation's linguistic resources (Zentella, "Language Minorities"). There can be no effective movement toward a language-competent society until this contradiction between the passionate cries for national foreign language competence and the callous indifference to maintaining the mother tongues of the nation's language minorities is resolved. If this contradiction is allowed to persist, the day may come when government and business executives lament the dearth of Spanish speakers in the U.S. Unthinkable? The same response was probably made about German less than seventy years ago.

But the members of U.S. English hasten to assure us that they are committed to foreign language education. We must ask, "What kind?" and "For whom?" In the past, as we have pointed out, those who fought to eradicate immigrant languages also tried to eliminate the study of foreign languages in the general population, thereby exposing their irrational fears. The proponents of the English-only amendment are more careful. Their tactics differ from those of their predecessors in that U.S. English, for example, advocates foreign language programs for "practical, economic, and foreign policy reasons," especially the study of critical languages (Pierce B4). This view divests the study of languages from its humanistic basis, and explicitly divorces it from the language strengths and needs of immigrants. It favors an enrichment approach to the education of monolingual English-speaking citizens but a subtractive, remediation approach for those who have another native language. Thus, the movement sustains an elitist posture regarding foreign language education, hoping to win converts within the ranks of language professionals. No English or foreign language educator should be deceived by such hypocrisy. The lessons of language history in the United States are too clear: any attack on the language rights of speakers of other languages does irreparable harm to the study of all languages, making it impossible to achieve a language-competent society, or an equitable society.

Why has an English-only movement resurfaced with such vigor at this time, and why is it so anti-Spanish? Again, history provides the answer. The acceptance of foreign languages in the U.S. has always waxed and waned in response to this country's sense of military and economic security and the need to accept or reject the nations or ethnic groups associated with the other languages (Macías). For example, the need to accommodate differences in the fledgling union led to greater linguistic tolerance on the part of the founders of the nation (Heath). Later, territorial expansion ran roughshod over native American lands and native American languages, and then slavery dismembered many African tribes and tongues. World War I created German scapegoats. In the last half of the twentieth century the problems presented by the economic and military significance of Latin America—problems unquestionably exacerbated by the unwelcome racial mixture of its many immigrants—make Spanish speakers the principal threat. When U.S. English warns that "circumstances . . . no longer favor assimilation in the majority culture" and lists ten "forces at work weakening the impulse toward assimilation" ("Frequently Used Arguments" 8), nine of these are anti-Hispanic. They range from the true, if obvious ("the nearness of the countries from which the migrants come" and "the growth of Spanish language communications"), to the wrong and dangerous ("the presence of a vocal Hispanic leadership which gives lip service to the need of Hispanics to learn English" and the "erosion of the moral position of those who urge the integration of Spanish speakers"). These attacks on the Hispanic community and its leadership are clear evidence of an anti-Latino paranoia which fosters racial and ethnic misunderstandings and even violence; indeed, violent attacks against Hispanics have been escalating recently.

The image of a Spanish-speaking community that "prefers not to speak English" (U.S. English, "Frequently Used Arguments" 8) and that could be readily assimilated and economically successful if only it learned to speak

English—otherwise "they never become productive members of American society" (Horn 1)—is completely at odds with the facts. The sad truth is that, despite the continued influx of monolingual immigrants which appears to slow down the process, Hispanics are undergoing language loss similar to that of other groups in U.S. history—the third generation is increasingly English monolingual. The 1980 census documents the fact that one-third of Hispanic children in the Southwest and one-fifth in New York are English-speaking monolinguals (Sole). Given the fact that almost one-half of all Hispanics in the U.S. are under the age of twenty and that 96 percent of the U.S. population speaks English, it seems obvious that, as the linguist G. Pullum observed, the English-only legislation "is as urgently called for as making hot-dogs the official food at baseball games" (608).

Another unfounded argument made in favor of the amendment concerns the link between proficiency and prosperity. Increased English proficiency has not led inevitably to greater economic security as claimed. New York Puerto Ricans speak 14 percent more English than other Hispanics but earn $4,200 less per annum (Mann and Salvo). Although their knowledge of English has continued to improve over the years, their economic situation has deteriorated. In 1970 Puerto Ricans earned 59 percent of the average U.S. income, whereas today they earn only 47 percent of the national average. Despite the lack of a positive correlation between greater English and greater income, which the experience of black and native Americans continues to corroborate, cities with large numbers of Puerto Ricans and other Hispanics have long waiting lists of adults seeking English classes—thirty to fifty thousand each in New York and Los Angeles alone (Nunberg cited in Crawford "Bilingual Education"). To meet this need, Hispanic legislators proposed an English Proficiency Act to provide for expanded English instruction; they asked the English-only organizations for support and received none. Instead, the most serious efforts that the community has made to learn English are attacked, not supported, by English-only advocates. Bilingual education is the most blatant example.

The most rigorous evaluations of bilingual education prove that it is more successful in teaching English than the submersion programs championed by English-only supporters (Hakuta and Gould). Yet ex-Senator Hayakawa, of U.S. English, maintains that bilingual education and bilingual ballots "threaten to divide us along language lines" ("Dear friend") and Texas Representative Horn, of English First, promises to "bring top experts to Capitol Hill to testify about the harmful consequences of bilingual ballots and bilingual education" (4). Instead, top experts meeting in December 1987 at Harvard's Institute on Bilingual Education cited research that documents the educational and cognitive benefits of bilingualism and true bilingual education programs (Bratt-Paulston, McLaughlin, Hakuta "Properties," Tucker, Snow). The unsubstantiated charges of U.S. English and English First are made at the expense of people who are overwhelmingly committed to learning English, as every study reveals, and who support bilingual education precisely because its primary goal is to teach English without allowing their children to fall behind academically. Moreover, these charges feed into linguistic myths about the nature of language-learning and the relationship of bilingualism to political stability, myths that must be laid to rest—especially by those of us who call ourselves linguists—because they breed intolerance.

Linguistic Myths Perpetuated

As suggested in our initial discussion of the dichotomous model perpetuated by English-only, one of the most damaging myths underlying the English language amendment is the idea that language-learning is a kind of hydraulic process—that there is room for mastery of only one language, as if languages competed for limited linguistic space in the brain (Hakuta *Mirror*). I believe this limited model leads people repeatedly to misinterpret a statement like "We want to keep our native language also" as "We don't want to learn English." Another implication of this approach is that bilingualism causes cognitive dissonance. Too many teachers continually tell parents that children will become confused if spoken to in more than one language. Linguistic research proves the contrary: not only can people learn a second language as competently as a native speaker, but proficiency in one's first language actually fosters the acquisition of English or any second language. Additionally, being bilingual has demonstrated cognitive assets, as Hakuta's research with lower-class children has substantiated.

Seemingly, all the research in the world will not convince those who prefer to deal in fear, not facts. Why else would the supporters of the ELA attribute political upheavals in different countries to the lack of an official language, when national fragmentation is inevitably the result of political and economic inequality? Surveys of nearly one hundred diverse nations corroborate the fact that it is not linguistic diversity that leads to instability but the lack of political and economic opportunities. Bilingualism may be a corrective in such situations. On the basis of a broad international perspective, Fishman concludes that "the problems popularly attributed to bilingualism are problems of social and economic development, control, and incorporation, superposed upon ethnolinguistic, racial, and religious differences. Without such superposition, problems of communication are solved, rather than created, by bilingualism"

("Bilingualism" 169). It is necessary to add that a nation with limited spheres of participation for its language minorities also fails to provide the atmosphere and opportunities necessary for learning the lingua franca. Even more damaging, repressive measures against language groups, such as the ELA, help ignite the fundamental socioeconomic and political tensions. They also backfire in another way, by increasing the ghettoization of language minorities and thus decreasing chances that these minorities will learn English.

Conclusion: Is Language the Real Issue?

I have attempted to summarize the most injurious repercussions of the misguided and unnecessary efforts to amend the U.S. Constitution to declare English the official language. The harmful fallout of the English-only movement is being felt already in communities where minority languages are spoken, but the proposed legislation holds negative consequences for all citizens, as well as for basic egalitarian principles. The impact on democracy in this country of the consequences of the law, if not of the seemingly innocuous wording of the amendment itself, overshadows any preoccupation with the lack of bilingual signs in Florida's zoos today or the challenges to driving examinations in North Carolina last year. Undeniably, Florida's current prohibition against bilingual prenatal services is cause for legitimate concern, and the prospect of legal impediments to providing preventive AIDS education in as many languages as necessary is terrifying. But even if exemptions were not allowed in areas of health and safety, the denial of services is less disturbing than the growing climate of intolerance spurred on by advocates of English-only. Belligerence towards speakers of other languages is reflected in everyday occurrences; for example, a supermarket clerk yelled "Speak English! This is America!" when I greeted another clerk in Spanish, and friends and students report similar incidents. These negative attitudes have permeated all levels of our society. Consider the outrageous response of Ohio State Representative Richard Rench to that state's Commission on Spanish-Speaking Affairs. When Commissioner Estrada respectfully wrote to Rench to "re-affirm our concern and ask that you reconsider your legislation [to make English the official language of Ohio]," the representative returned the letter stamped with a one-word reply—a profanity—which he labeled "very typical English." Not content to insult the commission and all the people it represents, in his defiant accompanying letter Rench urged, "if you are not happy with our United States of America, with English as its official language, you [should] consider moving to a country that does have an official language that makes you happy." Believing that both his interpretation of the reasons many question the legislation and his depatriation of all who disagree with him are inconsistent with the democratic principles he has sworn to uphold, Hispanic leaders in Ohio charged Rench with a violation of the code of ethics. Although individual members of the Ethics Committee "expressed concern over Representative Rench's use of the stamped expletive," the committee unanimously dismissed the charges against him.[3]

How does what starts out as an innocent "We just want to help everyone learn English so that we may communicate and they can succeed" turn into the odious impugning of the patriotism of those who support the rights of language minorities? The reason is that language is not the real issue but a smoke screen for the failure of the U.S. to resolve the inequality that exists; it is convenient to blame linguistic differences.[4] The root of the problem lies in an inability to accept an expanded definition of an American. The United States is no longer at the turn of the century when millions of European immigrants assimilated culturally and structurally, although many were never able to realize the American dream (Perlmann). The ELA says, "It worked for all the others" and "It will work for you." But it did not, and it will not. Today's newcomers are from distinct regions of a larger world, each at a different stage of development, and each group brings unique talents and troubles. The "browning" of America is underway; as the country changes what it looks like, so it must change how it looks at itself. Home is not where English speakers alone reside, and the American dream is not dreamt in English only. Home, and the heart of the American dream, are "life, liberty, and the pursuit of happiness." These are the principles on which we base our national unity, the principles which the Constitution must protect regardless of racial, cultural, and linguistic background. They have been challenged before; in 1780, John Adams proposed the establishment of a national language academy "to regulate and standardize English, but these efforts were rejected as out of keeping with the spirit of liberty in the U.S." (Heath 6). Do we believe more, or less, in that spirit 208 years later?

The presence of thirty-five million speakers of other languages requires us to answer that question honestly. Those in language-related professions, or in any of the humanities, might well be grateful to them for the chance to reexamine our values and our roles as teachers and researchers. The thoughtful reflection, evaluation of texts and facts, and elaboration of theories that are characteristic of our discipline can help us play a significant role in analyzing the present national language policy movement, if in the process we weigh the implications for those who may never enter a university or read a professional publication. When we consider the issues carefully, we realize how important is the value which the humanities have always placed upon the diversity of human life and experience. Then it is not enough to be against the English-only amendment; it is crucial to be clear about what we are *for*. The official-English movement labels diversity as a threat, when scholars in the humanities welcome it as an opportunity. We share a vantage point that should enable us to move beyond mere tolerance to acceptance and, ultimately, to the celebration of human diversity that the English-only movement decries.

Notes

1 The 1980 census data on Hispanics corroborate that "males, in general, were more likely to have a working knowledge of English," and that 44 percent of Puerto Rican families and 32 percent of Other Hispanic families have a female head of household. These families account for the majority of the over 47 percent of Puerto Rican households and 32 percent of Other Hispanic households who lived on less than $7,500 per year (Mann and Salvo 7).
2 See Lakoff; Thorne and Henley; Thorne, Kramarae, and Henley; McConnell-Ginet, Borker, and Furman; Penfield; Gershuny.
3 See Ethics Committee cited in *Unidad Borinqueña* 8.2 (1988): 1.
4 When the leadership of an anti-immigration organization (FAIR) sought the guidance of a marketing firm for the most effective way to encourage U.S. support for its cause, it was advised to concentrate on "they don't know English." A member of FAIR's board, John Tanton, became co-founder and chair of the board of U.S. English.

Bibliography

Beardsley, Theodore S., Jr. "Spanish in the United States." *The Spanish Language in the Western Hemisphere*. Ed. Eugene Chang-Rodríguez. Special issue of *Word* 33.1–2 (1982): 15–27.

Bratt-Paulston, Christina. "An International Perspective on Bilingualism and the Education of Language-Minority Children." Paper delivered at the Institute on Bilingual Education, Harvard University Graduate School of Education, 11 December 1987.

Butler, Rusty. *On Creating a Hispanic America: A Nation within a Nation?* Washington, D.C.: Council for Interamerican Security. 1985.

Combs, Mary Carol, and John Trasvina. "Legal Implications of the English Language Amendment." *The "English Plus" Project*. Washington, D.C.: League of United Latin American Citizens. June 1986.

Crawford, James. "Bilingual Education: Language, Learning, and Politics." *Education Week* 1 April 1987: 19–50.

_____. "Optimal Policies for Language-Minority Children." Paper delivered at the

Institute on Bilingual Education, Harvard University Graduate School of Education, 10 December 1987.

Estrada, Ramiro. Letter to State Representative Rench, 6 April 1987.

Fishman, Joshua A. "Bilingualism and Separatism." *Annals of the American Academy of Political and Social Sciences,* no. 487 (1986): 169–80.

———. " 'English Only': Its Ghosts, Myths and Dangers." Paper delivered at the California State Association for Bilingual Education annual meeting, 1987.

Gershuny, Lee. "Language and Feminist Research." *Women in Print I.* New York: Modern Language Association, 1986. 47–67.

Hakuta, Kenji. *Mirror of Language: The Debate on Bilingualism.* New York: Basic Books, 1986.

———. "Properties of the Bilingual Mind." Paper delivered at the Institute on Bilingual Education, Harvard University Graduate School of Education, 10 December 1987.

Hakuta, Kenji, and Laurie Gould. "Synthesis of Research on Bilingual Education." *Educational Leadership* 44 (March 1987): 38–45.

Hayakawa, S. I. "Dear friend." Fundraising letter for U.S. English. n.d.

———. "Questions Often Asked About State Campaigns to Make English Their Official Language." Manuscript. May 1987.

———. "Why the English Language Amendment." *English Journal.* December 1987: 14–16.

Heath, Shirley Brice. "English in our Language Heritage." *Language in the USA.* Ed. Charles Ferguson and Shirley Brice Heath. Cambridge: Cambridge University Press, 1981. 6–20.

Horn, Jim. "Dear Fellow American." Fundraising letter for English First. n.d.

Lakoff, Robin. *Language and Woman's Place.* New York: Harper Colophon Books, 1975.

Macías, Reynaldo. "Language Policy, Planning, and Politics in the United States Concerned with Language Minority Issues." *Annual Review of Applied Linguistics.* Rowley, Mass.: Newbury House, 1982. 86–104.

Mann, Evelyn S., and Joseph J. Salvo. "Characteristics of New Hispanic Immigrants to New York City: A Comparison of Puerto Rican and Non Puerto Rican Hispanics." *Research Bulletin: Hispanic Research Center.* Fordham University. Vol. 8, nos. 1–2:1–10.

McConnell-Ginet, Sally, Ruth Borker and Nancy Furman, eds. *Women and Language in Literature and Society.* New York: Praeger, 1980.

McLaughlin, Barry. "Language Acquisition in Bilingual and Incipiently Bilingual Children." Paper delivered at the Institute on Bilingual Education, Harvard University Graduate School of Education, 11 December 1987.

Penfield, Joyce, ed. *Women and Language in Transition.* Albany: SUNY, 1987.

Perlmann, Joel. "Bilingualism and Ethnicity in American Schooling before 1960: An Historical Perspective." Paper delivered at the Institute on Bilingual Education, Harvard University Graduate School of Education, 11 December 1987.

Pierce, N. "English as the Only U.S. Language." *Philadelphia Inquirer* 30 May 1983: B4.

Pullum, Geoffrey K. "Here Come the Linguistic Fascists." *Natural Language and Linguistic Theory* 5 (1987): 603–9.

Rench, Richard E. Letter to Director of Commission on Spanish-Speaking Affairs. 22 April 1987.

Simon, Paul. *The Tongue-Tied American: Confronting the Foreign Language Crisis.* New York: Continuum, 1980.

Snow, Catherine. "Determinants of School Achievement among Language-Minority Children." Paper delivered at the Institute on Bilingual Education, Harvard University Graduate School of Education, 12 December 1987.

Sole, Yolanda. "The Rise of Spanish." Paper delivered at the Symposium on Spanish and Portuguese Bilingualism, University of Colorado, Boulder, 31 October 1987.

Thorne, Barrie, and Nancy Henley, eds. *Language and Sex: Difference and Dominance.* Rowley, Mass.: Newbury House, 1975.

Thorne, Barrie, Cheris Kramarae and Nancy Henley, eds. *Language, Gender, and Society.* Rowley, Mass.: Newbury House, 1983.

Tucker, Richard. "Educational Programs for Language-Minority Children." Keynote Address delivered at the Institute on Bilingual Education, Harvard University Graduate School of Education, 10 December 1987.

U.S. English. "Fact Sheet: English Language Amendment." April 1987.

———. "Frequently Used Arguments Against the Legal Protection of English." n.d.

Zentella, Ana Celia. "Language Minorities and the National Commitment to Foreign Language Competency: Resolving the Contradiction." *ADFL Bulletin* 17, no. 3 (April 1986): 32–42.

———. "Language Variety among Puerto Ricans." *Language in the USA.* Ed. Charles Ferguson and Shirley Brice Heath. Cambridge: Cambridge University Press, 1981. 218–38.

of those that compose the New Right's infrastructure. In 1982, Ben Brodinsky reported that the New Right had "67 major national organizations" and "hundreds, possibly thousands" of local groups working on educational issues alone. Every thirty days, he stated, "the New Right creates a new organization . . . on national, state, or local levels."[3]

The leaders and organizations of the New Right are known for their vigorous action on a range of public issues. They are "militant opponents" of the Equal Rights Amendment, affirmative action, reproductive choice, unionism, federal social programs, government regulation of business and industry, the Panama Canal Treaty, and SALT II—activities for which they blame liberal humanists and politicians. They are "ardent proponents" of the Family Protection Act, the Human Life Amendment, prayer in public schools, the teaching of scientific creationism, parental censorship of school and library books, corporate "partnerships" with education, and increased defense spending.[4]

The New Right takes positions on these issues that may seem inconsistent to us until we view them through the lens of conservative ideology. To be against abortion and for nuclear proliferation, for instance, are contradictory positions if one values human life, but not if one fears human imperfection. These positions realign themselves coherently when they are taken *within* the reality erected by conservative ideology, which scholars usually describe as an amalgamation of capitalist economics, religious fundamentalism, and rampant individualism.[5] While I agree that the ideology combines these doctrines, I think it is important also to consider how it delineates human nature and society. It constitutes people as distinct individuals and society as an aggregation of individuals. It depicts all individuals as essentially imperfect (which is to say that they are self-interested according to the capitalist doctrine or fallen according to the fundamentalist one) and as determined, though differently so, on the basis of their sexes, races, and classes. The negativity of the New Right in attributing the problems of individuals to their sex or race, rather than to their social circumstances, is, of course, symptomatic of its sexism and racism but even more fundamentally of its profound pessimism about human nature. Tim LaHaye, for instance, says that "the best way to judge the quality of human nature is to examine what it does when it is free and unrestricted." Exemplifying human imperfection, he names Joseph Stalin, Mao Tse-tung, and the "humanist Adolf Hitler" on a list of evil dictators that contains no counter-examples (119). New Right ideology delineates a human nature that is radically essentialized and determined in its imperfections.

LaHaye infers pointedly, "Because man is not good by nature, a civilized culture must have moral laws based on biblical absolutes. Otherwise chaos will ensue" (214). The society that conservatives extrapolate from their version of human nature is marked by inequality, competition, and regulation, which furnish the structures and processes, respectively, for the social classes, the political economy, and the regulatory institutions. In other words, people are realized as classes (sex, race, class, etc.) of differently endowed individuals, who constitute the political economy as they compete for possession of resources, information, and power. Institutions, such as the family, church, school, and media, regulate these essentially imperfect and rampantly competitive individuals, providing cohesion to what otherwise would be an atomistic society. For the Christian Right, composed predominantly of Southern Baptists, Mormons, and other evangelical denominations, these particular versions of human nature and society were brought into existence by divine fiat. They are part of (not apart from, as liberal ideology has it) a transcendent order that exists in and beyond this world, before and after this time.[6]

When its strategies are seen as derived programmatically from this ideology, the New Right's issues and actions make sense in a way that the Left's issues and actions have not since the dissolution of the progressive coalition in the early 1970s and the subsequent divergence of feminist, liberal, radical left, and postmodern ideologies. From their ideology, conservatives derive their goals and then the organizations and strategies for attaining those goals. Given their instrumentalism, by which I mean their tendency to convert everything into the means to an end, I am less concerned about their ideology than about their strategies. In this essay, then, I review the strategies that propel them into a series of social actions from coalition-building to cultural reproduction and finally to ideological inversion.

First, the New Right uses the existing infrastructure of churches, Christian schools, evangelical television and radio networks, and single- and focused-issue groups in order to recruit diverse conservatives and then to integrate them organizationally. For instance, to mobilize conservative voters after Ronald Reagan's first nomination for the presidency, Moral Majority and Religious Roundtable, two New Right organizations, "geared up registration drives, urging ministers to get their congregants on the rolls. The typical device was to deputize a member of the congregation as registrar, who then enrolled voters at the church on Sunday morning. Moral Majority alone claimed to have registered between four and eight million new voters. . . . As Jerry Falwell explained, 'What can you do from the pulpit? You can register people to vote. You can explain the issues to them. And you can endorse candidates, right there in church on Sunday morning' " (Himmelstein 37). The founding of Moral Majority by Falwell, Greg Dixon, and Tim LaHaye itself is a classic demonstration of the strategic use of an infrastructure. They built this organization by creating a national network of fundamentalist ministers, who then used their churches, Christian schools, and media to form state chapters. Later, Religious Roundtable was founded by Ed McAteer, a Southern Baptist field organizer, as an umbrella organization to bring together leaders and personalities from the secular and Christian New Right and to attract the conservative clergymen who were not comfortable with either Christian Voice (an earlier coalition of special-interest groups) or Moral Majority.[7] "Modelled after industry's Business Roundtable" (Liebman 53), it conducted national seminars and coordinated its political activities with Moral Majority and Christian Voice. As Jerome Himmelstein observes, "what is new about the New Right is not its ideology, but its strategy of establishing linkages among a variety of conservative constituencies."[8]

Second, the New Right has become financially self-sustaining by using sophisticated fundraising techniques—computerization, direct mail, and mass media—to bring in small gifts that in total dollars far exceed the traditionally solicited large ones. Among the large contributors to a $1 billion campaign conducted in 1976–77 by the Rev. Bill Bright, founder of Campus Crusades for Christ and an early fundraiser for conservative causes, Nelson Bunker Hunt is reported to have donated $10 million personally and to have helped raise the rest, "much of it from large donors such as Pepsico, Mobil Oil, Coca-Cola, and the Adolph Coors family" (Liebman 51). As large as they seem, these contributions are exceeded annually by television and direct-mail solicitations. According to recent feature stories in *Time* and *Newsweek,* evangelical leaders raised $6 billion in 1987 through radio and television solicitations. Of this sum, $140 million were the revenues of Jimmy Swaggart, who reached between two and eight million viewers every Sunday, and $129 million were the revenues of M. G. (Pat) Robertson, a preacher and a candidate for the Republican presidential nomination in 1988.[9] Besides new technologies, the Right uses organizational entities in fundraising. When the Federal Election Campaign Act of 1974 limited individual contributions to $1,000, conservatives moved faster than other constituencies in establishing Political Action Committees (PACs) to raise and distribute money. A share of the money raised by all these means supports conservative Christian schools, colleges, and seminaries.

Third, the New Right can perpetuate its human resources. By developing systems of primary, secondary, higher, and seminary education, by offering community education in churches and other venues, and by sponsoring political workshops, it trains its members and—even more important—wins young hearts and minds. In *Listen, America,* his cry to rally sixty million Americans "who profess to be born-again Christians" and another sixty million "who consider themselves religious promoralists,"[10] Jerry Falwell criticizes secondary and higher education for its godless humanism, antireligious textbooks, sexual anarchy, violence, and vandalism.[11] Under these circumstances, he writes, Christian parents choose to educate their children in Christian schools, which afford "the only hopes of training young men and young women who will be capable of taking the helm of leadership in every level of society." Falwell reports that the "14,000 conservative Christian schools" in existence by 1980 were "increasing at a rate of three per day" (219). His figures have proved to be only slightly higher than the actual increase of two per day during the subsequent five years. For 1985, James Davison Hunter, a sociologist, places the number of evangelical schools "between 17,000 and 18,000, representing roughly two and a half million students. This growth," he points out, "is occurring in a climate of sharply declining educational enrollment."[12] Conservative Christian colleges, universities, and seminaries are also growing in number and size. According to data for 1981–82, Hunter estimates 773 religiously affiliated colleges and universities, of which approximately 100 meet the Christian College Coalition criteria for evangelical institutions (243). For 1986–87, the *Reader's Digest Almanac* lists approximately 882 religiously affiliated institutions, of which some 255 are fundamentalist or conservative Christian.[13] The increased numbers and sizes of institutions are part of what conservative writers perceive to be a national "reconstruction of Christian higher education" during the 1970s and 1980s (Ringenberg 188).[14]

But the New Right does not confine its educational endeavors to schools. As early as 1979, a feminist "mole" at the Republican National Committee headquarters in Washington, D.C. reported that conservatives were providing two-week political action training programs in the nation's capital for teams of would-be local and state conservative activists.[15] More recently, according to Margaret Ann Latus, the four prominent conservative Political Action Committees she studied—but not four comparable liberal ones—conducted schools for political candidates and workshops on political action for church and community groups.[16] The inventiveness of the New Right in choosing venues of education reminds me of the injunction voiced by a black activist in the 1970s. "Never," she said, "miss an opportunity to educate." To educate, the New Right uses schools, sermons, televangelism, even direct mail. Richard Viguerie knows better than anyone how direct mail is used not only to raise money but also to propagate ideas and recruit activists. Latus elaborates the point: "A complete direct mail package can educate individuals on political issues, can advertise the merits of the soliciting agency, promote feelings of identification and membership with the cause, and encourage other grassroots political activities, as well as request contributions" (82).

Fourth, the New Right is attempting to extricate itself from the external regulations that radicalized it in the first place. Conservatives experienced federal intervention in education—for instance, the teaching of evolution in the 1940s and 1950s, the abolition of school prayer in 1962, affirmative action and busing during the 1970s—as the intrusions of liberal humanism into their beliefs and lives, but these intrusions were symptomatic of the deeper problem. The liberal humanism purveyed in public institutions seemed to the Christian Right to be "characterized by godlessness, moral relativism, and permissiveness regarding decency issues."[17] Convinced that liberal humanism "has twisted the First Amendment to mean the separation of God from government and society" (Heinz 134) and appalled to find education responsive to special interest groups (such as women, minorities, and the handicapped), the New Right is trying to abolish the roles of government as a regulator and as a provider of public education by placing this education in a market economy where it will compete with other types of education. At the same time, as the *Grove City College* case suggests, the Right is using the courts, legislatures, and agencies to challenge the federal regulations that apply to conservative institutions and to disconnect these regulations from the tax-exempt status and federal funds that its institutions receive.[18]

Fifth, in opposition to liberal humanism, the Christian Right is inverting the liberal separation of church and state. Liberal ontology radically differentiates the supernatural and the mundane. Liberals bar religious beliefs and practices from the public domains of education, politics, society, and even civic space; and in academic inquiry they reject supernatural explanations for natural phenomena. Fundamentalist ontology radically integrates the mundane into the supernatural. Fundamentalists locate all public and private activities within divine time and space; and in academic inquiry, as in everything else, they impose religious and teleological explanations. The Christian Right sees liberalism as a religion that arrogantly denies theocentric reality, while liberalism, of course, denies that it is religious, let alone ideological.

Tim LaHaye's *The Battle for the Mind,* an account of the ultimate struggle between liberal humanism and conservative Christianity, exemplifies the technique of inversion. In a chapter provocatively titled "Humanism Is a Religion," LaHaye marshals stray remarks from various sources—*the Humanist Manifesto I* and *II,* the Supreme Court case of *Torcaso* v. *Watkins,* and an uncited debate by Thomas Jefferson—to argue that liberal humanism is a religion based reprehensibly on "Disbelief in God," "Deification of man as supreme," "Rejection of absolute morals," and "Belief in the innate goodness of men to govern the world equitably" (130). Once he has made an ideology a religion, he laments that this religion has become a national one. The Christian Right, he claims, was fooled into accepting the dubious political doctrine that religion should not enter politics at the very moment that the liberal humanists had infiltrated the federal government and gained control of education. "Since the educational system has been taken over by humanism, and since humanism is an officially declared religion, we find the government establishing a religion and giving the high priest a position in the president's cabinet. Ironically, the taxes to pay for the establishment of such a godless religion come from people who are overwhelmingly God conscious and pro-moral" (211). New Right leaders like LaHaye use a conservative interpreta-tion of belief systems to define liberal humanism as a religion and a liberal interpretation of the separation of church and state to argue against the pro-mulgation of liberal humanism by educational institutions. Thus when Jerry Falwell says, " 'We strongly oppose the teaching of the religion of secular [*i.e.*, liberal] humanism in the public school classroom' " (Brodinsky 90), we know that he, too, views all belief systems as religions and that he is attempt-ing strategically to use the separation of church and state doctrine to abolish this one.

Liberals, for the most part, have not understood the inversion that conser-vative Christians are trying to effect, and they continue to interpret the mixing of religion and politics as a civic impropriety. Consequently, they were shocked when the Christian Right held a prayer breakfast at the 1984 Re-publican National Convention in Dallas and President Reagan attended it, because they thought that the New Right had imported religion into the do-main of public politics.[19] Far more insidiously, however, the New Right is transforming political practice into religious practice by using churches and clergy to register voters, educate congregants on political issues, and train them to be political activists. When I say "transforming," I speak from a perspective that differs from the liberal one, for I do not believe that the influence between religion and politics can be blocked. To liberals, conser-vative Christianity should exist apart from the nation. To fundamentalists, the nation should exist in conservative Christianity. To me, the nation and conser-vative Christianity are presently being employed to reconstitute each other.

New Right Organizing

The New Right has been enormously effective in applying these strategies to its various activities—building organizations, raising funds, lobbying, cam-paigning, and making social change. The building of Moral Majority, the largest conservative organization, is a case in point. Founded in June 1979 by three fundamentalist clergymen, Jerry Falwell, Tim LaHaye, and Greg Dixon, Moral Majority actually consists of four organizations: (1) Moral Ma-jority, Inc., a tax-exempt lobby that attempts to influence national, state, and local legislation; (2) Moral Majority Foundation, a tax-deductible fund that educates ministers and lay people about political issues and conducts voter registration drives; (3) Moral Majority Legal Defense Fund, a tax-deductible opponent of the American Civil Liberties Union (ACLU) that has vowed "to battle humanism through the courts" (Liebman 54); and (4) Moral Majority PAC, established to support conservative political campaigns. The organization was built expansively and rapidly. Two years after its founding, Moral Majority was spending $6 million annually, mostly on media campaigns. It published *Moral Majority Report,* which reached 840,000 homes and approximately three million readers, and broadcast a daily commentary on 300 radio stations. Its leaders claimed a membership of four million Americans, while outsiders estimated its membership at 400,000 (Liebman 55).

How was this organization built? Its three founders each headed a fundamentalist empire. Jerry Falwell is pastor of the 21,000-member Thomas Road Baptist Church in Lynchburg, Virginia, and broadcasts a weekly service on 373 television stations. He is chancellor of three institutions of higher education—Liberty University, Liberty Baptist Seminary, and Liberty Home Bible Institute—and a member of innumerable conservative boards. Tim LaHaye, founder of San Diego Christian Unified School System and of Christian Heritage College, has written "at least sixteen books which sell more than 300,000 copies a year" and conducts Family Life Seminars with his wife Beverly, who herself heads "a national prayer chain with more than 94,000 members" (Liebman 59). Greg Dixon, founder of the 8,000-member Indianapolis Baptist Temple, organized rallies and fought conservative political battles during the 1970s. Personally, these three men brought their geographical diversity, strategic experience, and access to an infrastructure to bear in the task of building a national organization.

Falwell, LaHaye, and Dixon designed a Moral Majority that had a national headquarters (an office in Washington and board of directors) and fifty state chapters. The men chosen to lead these chapters shared the profile of the founders: fifty were clergymen; twenty-eight belonged to the Baptist Bible Fellowship, a confederation of 2,500 fundamentalist churches that supports Baptist Bible College, "which bills itself as the world's largest Bible college" (Liebman 66); at least twenty-five sponsored Christian schools; and most were involved in conservative issues and campaigns. As Liebman says, "the leadership of Moral Majority recruited men most like themselves. Their success in starting state chapters depended on the conjunction of shared identity and common organization. The presence of a national network of fundamentalist clergy united by a common fellowship, attendance at a small number of Bible colleges, a commitment to building churches and Christian schools, and prior experience in fundamentalist political crusades made rapid mobilization possible" (68–69).

During the 1980 presidential election, the state chapters of Moral Majority followed the directive of the national organization to register conservative voters, capture the delegate-selection process, and support conservative candidates. After the election, the state chapters returned to their work on various issues—for instance, opposition to gay rights bills in Minnesota and California; anti-abortion legislation in Ohio, Arizona, Connecticut, Idaho, Maryland, New Jersey, New York, and Washington; and legislation authorizing the teaching of scientific creationism in the schools of Arkansas, Illinois, Louisiana, Oregon, and Washington (Liebman 71). Not only the rapidity with which Moral Majority was built but also the scope of its concerns and its fluidity in addressing them are remarkable feats of organizing. Liebman believes that Moral Majority's success in "wielding disparate local activities and activists into a national movement" was its use of an existing infrastructure of clergy, churches, schools, colleges, and media. But "the centerpiece of its mobilization campaign," he points out, "was the local church" (72). In its organizing, as in its ideologizing, the New Right is staunchly theocentric.

The Conservative Agendas for Higher Education

Education is important to liberals, leftists, and conservatives for different reasons. To liberals, education matters materially; it is a means to production, acquisition, and status. They turn to it for the credentials that give them access to careers and income. To leftists, education matters functionally; it is an apparatus of ideological and cultural (re)production. They develop a critique of the educational agents and institutions that fuel this (re)production. To conservatives, education matters strategically; it is an instrument to be used in the ultimate struggle against liberal humanism to own America. Given their sense of urgency, conservatives draw up an action-agenda for education. Or to put the distinction bluntly, while the radical Left analyzes, the radical Right acts. What guides its action?

At present, most observers of conservatism distinguish between the centrist and radical Right agendas for education. The centrist agenda, formulated by neoconservatives, some traditional liberals, and policy analysts at the American Enterprise Institute, finds that "federal intervention to promote educational equity was excessive" both in placing equity before excellence and in pursuing it " 'with almost no regard to the financial costs involved.' "[20] It specifies reordering the goals of public education so that they first *promote economic growth* for the nation," then "help *preserve a common culture* by teaching students the basic values upon which American capitalism is based," and finally support educational equity (Pincus 52). They want to redefine, not abolish, the federal role in education and to supplement it with "cooperation between business and education" (Pincus 52, 53). Former Secretary of Education Terrel H. Bell, who reduced federal support of education, and Professor E. D. Hirsch, Jr., who hopes to preserve a common culture by enforcing cultural literacy, each enact this agenda.

By his own account, Bell sought to implement the centrist agenda during his tenure as Secretary of Education. In "Education Policy Development in the Reagan Administration," the apologia he wrote after leaving his post, Bell describes the attack of the radical Right on his goals. These he represents as more moderate than President Reagan's goals, which were to reduce federal spending for and involvement in education, "to strengthen local and state control," to increase parental choice among schools and school competition for students, and "to abolish the U.S. Department of Education,"[21] perhaps replacing it with "a foundation similar to the National Science Foundation, but with a less powerful board" (489). The radical Right had powerful allies on the White House senior staff and in the Office of Management and Budget who opposed Bell, and they had nationally organized "zealots" who directed "vile and compassionless diatribes" at government liberals and moderate conservatives alike (Bell 488, 490). They fought Bell because he wished to preserve the Department of Education, although in attenuated form, and would not eliminate all student aid and affirmative action programs. Arguing that public education was tied "to a strong economy and national security" (490), he wanted the public and private sectors to support the management of education by states and localities. Struggling against these groups within the administration and without, wavering between praise for the president's tolerance of dissent among his Cabinet officers and criticism of his failure to formulate a coherent education policy, the beleaguered Bell ends his story happily by explaining how, through his position and wit, he was able to rescue the Department of Education from extinction.[22]

In several articles and a book published since 1980, E. D. Hirsch, Jr., has appeared to advocate the preservation of a common culture by installing a core curriculum in schools and universities. Recently, he argued in a *Salmagundi* forum that he has been misunderstood. In response to Robert Scholes's charge that he is attempting "to impose a canon on all humanistic study in this country,"[23] Hirsch argues that "cultural literacy is a canon of information, not of texts," and that "true [cultural] literacy requires widely shared background knowledge."[24] Pointing out their deficiencies in this information, Hirsch cites national samples showing the large numbers of 17-year-olds who do not know the dates of the Civil War, the names of standard British and American authors, the meaning of the term "Reconstruction," and the identity of Stalin or Churchill. Then he makes an unwarranted leap in logic. "No knowledgeable reading researcher," he says, "disputes the fact that a higher level of national literacy will come only through a higher level of nationally shared information" (124). Defending the centrist agenda against liberal criticism, Hirsch has imperceptibly extended its cultural penetration: what gets imposed on school children has gone from a canon of texts to a core curriculum and now, in his latest rendition, to a canon of information. Information of the sort that Hirsch has in mind in his highly publicized list of "What Literate Americans Know"[25] is expressed in our culture not by school curricula alone but by all the media capable of expressing it—presumably newspapers, pledges of allegiance, rock videos, family conversations, museum exhibitions, exchanges in the corner grocery, TV sit-coms, and subway posters. In other words, the content is extremely selective, the means for instilling it extremely pervasive. The implicit totalitarianism of his vision is stunning. But if conservatives do control all these media so that they express a common culture, which culture would they express? Will the common culture be black culture? Will it even include black culture? If the centrist agenda is implemented, I expect not.

The radical Right agenda, articulated by fundamentalists and policy analysts at the Heritage Foundation, finds that by monopolizing university faculties and federal agencies liberal humanists have controlled education "to the detriment of quality teaching and academic standards."[26] It proposes to disassemble the federal role in education—including abolishing the Department of Education, eliminating federal funding of education, and reducing civil rights regulations and enforcement—and to make education responsive to market forces. *A New Agenda for Education,* the slim volume published by the Heritage Foundation in 1985, adds to these goals the elimination of university departments of education (80) and the approval of direct contractual arrangements whereby universities could do research for federal agencies. At the same time, radical Right scholars and educators have undertaken the hard work of building conservative Christian higher education. As Nathan O. Hatch argues in "Evangelical Colleges and the Challenge of Christian Thinking," "the battle for the mind" will not be fought only "by mobilizing in the streets or on Capital Hill, nor by denouncing more furiously the secular humanists. If we are to help preserve even the possibility of Christian thinking for our children and grandchildren, we must begin to nurture first-order Christian scholarship . . . [which] is still vitally important if evangelicals today are to be able to establish a beachhead, however tiny, in territory that has become pervasively alien during the last century."[27]

The activities of William J. Bennett, first as chairman of the National Endowment for the Humanities (NEH) and later as Secretary of Education, have been calculated to advance the radical Right agenda. An accomplished ideologue and strategist, Bennett has reiterated a cluster of themes—that we need certainty, coherence, and authority in knowledge; that we have relativism, fragmentation, and moral failure—in such publications as "The Shattered Humanities," an article that appeared in the *Wall Street Journal,* and "To Reclaim a Legacy," a report released by NEH. These pieces outline his educational ideology, goals, and strategies. In the first piece, Bennett fears that the term *humanities* is "becoming meaningless" because "the studies we associate with the humanities no longer stand for a unified set of principles or a coherent body of knowledge. The disciplines . . . have become frighteningly fragmented, even shattered. Rigorous modes of inquiry in organized fields of knowledge have been replaced by a jumble of indiscriminate offerings."[28] He experiences this diversity in knowledge negatively as degeneration rather than positively as recuperation. Its cause, he believes, is the liberal fascination with relativism, but he has an odd understanding of relativism:

> I recently read an article by several college administrators asserting, in a self-congratulatory way, that the proper aim of their general education program was to encourage students to think relativistically. . . . But what is the promise, the hope, the high end of an education that urges students to think that all ideas have the same value? Why would one bother? . . . I am reminded of a student I recently met who told me that he wasn't taking any religion courses at his university because no one in the religion department believed anything, and he wasn't taking any philosophy courses because no one in the philosophy department recommended anything. Students want and need to know where educated people stand, not on passing issues but on matters of enduring importance, matters that always have been the concern of the humanities: courage, fidelity, friendship, honor, love, justice, goodness, ambiguity, time, power, faith. ("Shattered Humanities" 10)

To Bennett, relativism means abstaining from making value judgments, having no values, not taking positions, lacking belief, being faithless. To relativists, it means that people have and do all of these things *only* and *always* within particular contexts, so that everybody's values, judgments, positions, and beliefs are contingent. The contingency of knowledge is what Bennett resists, the authority of tradition what he wishes to restore.

In "To Reclaim a Legacy," a report on the state of the humanities in higher education, Bennett argues that the humanities as traditionally represented and studied are an "unclaimed legacy," "a heritage" that "educators . . . have given up the task of transmitting . . . to its rightful heirs."[29] He defines the humanities first by listing disciplines and then by describing the objects they study as "landmarks of human achievement" (17) and "masterworks of English, American, and European literature" and art (18). Paraphrasing Matthew Arnold on quality, he declares them "the best that has been said, thought, written, and otherwise expressed about human experience" (17). In order to select the best objects, educators must have "a clear vision of what is worth knowing" (17), apply standards, and make judgments. These humanities, defined as a specially valued collection of disciplinary objects, are to form "a core of common studies" (16) that will "contribute to [our] informed sense of community" and enable us to "become participants in a common culture, shareholders in our civilization" (17). Through the imposition of these common studies, Bennett hopes to restore certainty and authority to a domain of knowledge balkanized by relativism. His need for these conditions is nowhere more obvious than in the sentence which introduces his own list of masterworks: "The works and authors I mention virtually define the development of the Western mind" (18). *The works and authors* is a limited set. *Define,* the act of limiting and characterizing, is what they do. *The Western mind* that they define is a single mind, further delimited as a Western typification. In this sentence, Bennett shuts out diversity and relativity because for him the restoration of valuable property is the ostensible aim.

Bennett's strategic reason for wanting certainty and authority in knowledge is, of course, to transfer decision making about higher education from liberals to conservatives. He hopes to accomplish this shift (1) by installing a core curriculum that would in effect obviate the need for decision making by the now diverse constituents of higher education, (2) by using the media to leverage public opinion against liberal higher education, and (3) by disposing of federal funding to erode liberal higher education. The public opinion strategy may be deduced with nice reflexivity from media reports on Bennett. According to the May 7, 1986, issue of *The Chronicle of Higher Education,* the Department of Education reduced the travel funds allotted to civil rights investigators but increased those allotted Bennett for FY 1987. His travel budget of $200,000, which more than doubled the amount spent in 1985, was 25 percent of the civil rights travel budget of $801,000, which represents a 13 percent decrease from 1985. Where did he travel, and why? According to his schedule for April 1986, which was reprinted in the *Chronicle,* he made eleven trips, almost all of them to conservative regions of the country and to conservative institutions, including Wake Forest University, Jerry Falwell's Liberty University, and the National Catholic Educational Association.[30] As to why he made these trips, the *Chronicle* quoted Bennett responding in the third person: "It has been very educational for the Secretary to go where he has been going and to see the things he sees" (13). Does the secretary really hope to persuade the American people that a government official should put his personal edification before a public benefit like civil rights evaluation and enforcement? More reasonably, the explanation is a pretext for the real purpose of travel: it provides occasions when the secretary can persuade the American people of his educational views.

Indeed, six months later, the *Chronicle* carried another story, this one titled

"A Finely Tuned Public-Relations Effort Keeps Bennett in the Public Eye." It reported that Bennett, who was "one of the most visible members of President Reagan's Cabinet," "made three television appearances last month, had interviews with seven journalists, and held press conferences after almost every speech he delivered."[31] The article went on to recount the strategies that obtained the media coverage and was accompanied by two more articles on the personnel who assist him: the recently appointed director of the Department of Education's Public Affairs Office, and the department's press secretary who changed Bennett's image. "Previous Secretaries," the article stated, "worked closely with higher education representatives and discussed ways that together they could solve the problems facing academe. Mr. Bennett rarely talks to those representatives," but instead uses the media, he says, " 'to have a conversation with the American people about education' " (17). This secretary has not worked closely with education representatives because they strenuously oppose the radical Right agenda that he is trying to implement.

The same strategic sense that Bennett shows in using the media to leverage popular opinion against liberal higher education is at work in his attempts to dispose of federal funding in ways that erode liberal higher education. The Fund for the Improvement of Postsecondary Education (FIPSE), which is housed in the Department of Education, is a case in point. In February 1985, President Reagan's budget for FY 1986 "proposed to eliminate the $12.7 million agency."[32] During the summer, Bennett tried to transfer FIPSE from the jurisdiction of one assistant secretary to that of another but met with pressure from Congress and educational associations. In the fall, he proposed to change the rules governing its awards. Although FIPSE had "not previously issued official guidelines about the kinds of projects that it [was] willing to support," Bennett announced that its highest priority would be to support projects that encouraged the " 'renewal of the undergraduate curriculum based on a clearly articulated vision of the knowledge and skills an educated person should possess, and on the intellectual heritage of Western civilization' " (15). It would no longer support projects designed to "increase access to higher education for minority groups and disadvantaged students" (15). A month later, in October 1985, Bennett fired the director of FIPSE because, sources said, "he had been too outspoken in his criticisms of the Secretary's proposals to change the way the fund operates."[33] At the same time that he replaced this director with a longtime friend and advisor, he made five appointments to the national board of the fund. Among them was a philosophy professor who had served on the study group that advised Bennett on "To Reclaim a Legacy," the report which described the very curriculum that Bennett was now trying to use FIPSE funding to install.[34]

The Conservative Transformation of Liberal Higher Education

Former Secretary Terrell H. Bell aptly paraphrases the priorities of the radical Right agenda: the defunding of education and the creation of an educational marketplace:

> The true movement conservatives believe that not a dime of federal money should be spent on education. . . . Some members of the movement would also relieve state and local government of any role in education. Their rationale is that a school district is a government-operated monopoly, and that is the worst type of monopoly imaginable.
>
> Let the marketplace supply education to the consumer, they say. . . . Let the free enterprise system work to provide education. Let entrepreneurs establish schools and compete for the market. The marketplace will discipline and weed out the inefficient and less efficient. (Bell 491)

The discourse these conservatives employ when they talk about defederalizing education reveals their possessive strategy. First, when they say that federally supported education is a government monopoly, they mean that this education is purveying one kind of product—a kind they do not want to purchase or consume. That product is liberal humanism, and they do not want public funds to subsidize it. Thus they oppose federal "appropriations to the National Science Foundation," because " 'most of these funds are used to stack the ideological deck in favor of Godless behavioral humanist research which contradicts the Christian viewpoint of mankind's nature' " (Liebman 53). The New Right understands what Mary O'Brien points out in "Feminism and the Politics of Education." In democratic states, which "rely on the consent of the governed," she writes, educational institutions engage in "the manufacturing of such consent" (100). According to radical Right discourse, our institutions manufacture consent to live in godlessness.[35]

Consequently, New Right leaders are attempting to transform education from a not-for-profit service to a marketplace of competing educational institutions: public and private, Christian and secular. They believe that if these institutions are placed in a market economy, they will be controlled by those who can direct the market—the capitalists and consumers of education—and they have reasonable hopes that those who can direct the market will be themselves. As consumers of education, conservatives are actively seeking seats on school boards, joining such groups as Accuracy in Academe, and pressuring textbook publishers. As capitalists, they are obtaining education degrees, entering the professions of teaching and administration, and establishing independent schools to compete with public ones. To increase the susceptibility of educational institutions to market forces, conservatives have proposed financial measures, such as tuition tax credits and vouchers, that will give consumers more power to pressure these institutions.

The transformation of education from a publicly supported service to a marketplace has another effect: it undercuts our professionalism as educators, our authority to produce knowledge, train and evaluate fellow professionals, and regulate our profession. In an article for the Heritage Foundation portentously titled "The Demise of the Teaching Profession," Annette and Russell Kirk report that parents and legislators have "declared [their] displeasure with the present state of 'teacher recruitment, selection, training, certification, competency, and licensing.' "[36] Later they add teachers' unions, tenure, and salary to this list of items that the New Right hopes to regulate for educators. Conservative leaders are not the only people who understand that professionalism enables the monopoly of a discipline or service. Marxist and feminist authors provide the analyses. In *The Rise of Professionalism: A Sociological Analysis,* Magali Sarfatti Larson points out that professions have become special, valued, and monopolistic occupations because professionals can control their ideologies, training, and markets. They gain professional autonomy because they are "allowed to define the very standards by which [their] superior competence is judged." But these privileges also create problems. First, professionals are apt to "live within ideologies of their own creation, which they present to the outside as the most valid definitions of specific spheres of social reality." Moreover, the very autonomy they experience through their ability to control their profession tends to blind them to the fragility of that autonomy.[37] Controlling educational standards and markets is what New Right professionals aim to do as they write critically about liberal educational standards and markets. Whether we recognize this move depends upon the extent to which we believe in our own ideology and autonomy.

The New Right is not opposed to professionalism *per se.* Conservative Christians, who historically have had a lower educational and socioeconomic status than most other segments of the population, now increasingly receive higher educations and move into the professional classes (Hunter 11). Aiding this movement, conservative Christian higher education employs the discourse of professionalism in its documents and emphasizes professional training. Students who major in theology often take a second major in a profession, such as Christian education, social work, mass media, or business administration. The education of students in baccalaureate and professional programs occurs now, according to historians, only because since the 1960s many conservative Christian colleges and universities have undergone institution-wide professionalization in the form of the credentialing of faculty, the accreditation of programs, and the specialized training of administrators.[38]

The New Right is opposed only to liberal or secular professions and eager to turn professionalism to its own purposes.

In the context of an educational marketplace, Bennett's recent proposal for student aid would produce unprecedented conservative change. Criticizing colleges and universities for a decade of tuition increases, he claimed that government loans to students do "*not* make it easier for families to meet college costs. Rather, in the end, more loan money makes it easier for colleges to *raise* college costs."[39] Although he agreed to retain programs that aid the neediest students, he wanted to overhaul other student aid programs by eliminating government loan subsidies and placing more responsibility for repayment on students. In addition, he proposed to restrict federal aid to students at institutions that increase their tuitions more than 1 percent beyond the annual inflation rate. Bennett declared that new policies along these lines would create the pressure that was needed to help colleges and universities refrain from making unnecessary tuition increases. "If the students paid the full costs of borrowing, he said, they would become more demanding consumers" of the education they received (Evangelauf 21).

Opponents of Bennett's proposal criticize the damage it will do to lower income and minority students. Indeed, an article titled "Affirmative Action on Campus" reports that similar policies are having these effects: "Already, the number of minority students entering colleges and universities has sharply declined. The decline in minority undergraduate enrollment has been blamed on the Reagan administration's federal aid program cuts, recruitment difficulties, and, according to Edward Fiske, 'a lessened commitment to the affirmative action programs that, in the early 1970s, brought swiftly rising numbers of minority students to the nation's campuses.' Likewise, recent drops in graduate enrollment at universities like Stanford, Michigan, University of California at Berkeley, Princeton, Harvard, and Columbia will mean a decline in available minority faculty five years hence."[40]

But in an educational marketplace, Bennett's proposal could precipitate an even larger demographic shift. The tuitions charged by conservative Christian colleges and universities are generally lower than those charged by other private colleges and universities in the same or comparable states. For instance, *The College Blue Book* for 1987 lists costs (tuition, room, board, and fees for out-of-state students) of $9,800 for the Southern Baptist–affiliated Wake Forest University and $14,201 for the private Duke University, both in North Carolina. Similarly, costs are $5,850 for the small Southern Baptist Mars Hill College in North Carolina; $10,380 for Randolph-Macon Woman's College in Lynchburg, Virginia; and $11,900 for Hollins College in Hollins, Virginia. This disparity is even greater when geography is considered. Most conservative Christian universities are located in low-cost regions of the South and

Midwest, whereas most comparable private universities are located in higher-cost regions of the Northeast and Midwest. Among universities with 4,000 to 5,000 students, Bob Jones University of South Carolina charges $5,160 and Oral Roberts University of Oklahoma charges $5,871, whereas Tufts University in Massachusetts charges $9,562 and Butler University in Indiana charges $9,710. The fundamentalist Liberty University in Virginia, which has over 6,000 students, charges $3,210 for tuition and fees while Suffolk University in Massachusetts charges $5,851 for the same.[41] Conservative Christian institutions can charge lower tuitions because their own expenditures are generally lower in two major areas of any institutional budget—faculty compensation and physical plant (including utilities)—and because they receive income from profit-making units, such as radio and television stations. In such a marketplace, consumers are not likely to choose those which charge the highest tuition and offer the least federal aid. Under Bennett's proposal, it is mainly our secular institutions that would lose students to the conservative ones and would suffer reductions in federal student aid.

The Fundamentalist Takeover of Conservative Christian Higher Education

The Southern Baptist Convention, which is the leading confederation in this denomination, controls six theological seminaries and, with state conventions, supports several colleges and universities. Since 1979, the fundamentalists have defeated the moderates in electing presidents of the national convention, and these presidents have been replacing the moderates on institutional boards. The election in June 1986 of the fundamentalist Rev. Adrian P. Rogers, observers predicted, "insures three more years of fundamentalist appointments—enough to clinch at least a simple majority on virtually every board."[42] According to the *Chronicle of Higher Education*, "the fundamentalists . . . have stated that two of their goals are to root out faculty members and administrators in the seminaries who do not share their views and to change practices in the seminaries that they consider heretical" ("After Election" 1, 24). In the subsequent year and a half, fundamentalists have instigated takeovers of North Carolina's Southeastern Baptist Theological Seminary, where they precipitated the resignations of President W. Randall Lolley and Dean Morris J. Ashcraft, and of Mercer University, the second largest Baptist university in the nation, where they accused President R. Kirby Godsey of heresy and the student body of drunkenness, obscene language, and lewd behavior.[43] Not very reassuringly, the Reverend Mr. Rogers was quoted as saying, " 'We're not trying to tell any professor what he must believe—that is between him and God. . . . But we are saying that those who work for us and who have their salaries paid by us ought to reflect what the great majority of us say we want taught' " ("After Election" 24). He added "that there was a 'danger' in looking at seminaries 'from a university perspective,' as 'places of inquiry where we are delving into more esoteric areas of truth' " and admitted that " 'basically I think of our seminaries as training schools, very similar to a trade school.' "[44] Indeed, my study of fundamentalist college, university, and seminary bulletins reveals that these institutions are devoted to inculcating doctrine and training.

Fundamentalist institutions, by definition, subordinate their educational mission to a religious one. Typical of the sixty-three institutions described in the conservative Christian College Coalition's *A Guide to Christian Colleges* (1982), Trinity College in Deerfield, Illinois, makes this statement: "Trinity College realizes that the foundation of all knowledge is Jesus Christ. All truth is God's truth, and at the center of all that is undertaken by participants in the College community is the belief in the centrality of Jesus Christ in every aspect of thought and life."[45] In effecting the integration of knowledge into religion, all the institutional resources are brought to bear. For the conservative Christian college, writes William C. Ringenberg, "it is not enough to publish doctrinal statements, hold chapel services, and require Bible courses; rather the whole program must radiate the Christian faith. As William Clark has said, 'The Christian college does not have a religious program; it is a religious program' " (Ringenberg 215). And yet for all its doctrinal uniformity, the Christian college is a religious program whose beliefs must get imposed, as Alan Peshkin remarked of the fundamentalist school he studied (90–110), by an elaborate structure of controls that includes the frequent avowal and enforcement of allegiance.

Most of the seventy institutions that belong to the Christian College Coalition require students, faculty, and administrators to subscribe to articles of faith (Hunter 168). The "Personal Word From the President," which appears in the bulletin of Bob Jones University, a fundamentalist institution with 4,039 students and 332 faculty in Greenville, South Carolina, is typical of the statements that appear in the bulletins of these institutions: "Religiously, our testimony is, 'Whatever the Bible says is true.' Standing firmly for and contending aggressively for the great Fundamentals of Christian Faith, Bob Jones University is proud to be known as Fundamentalist in its position. We oppose all atheistic, agnostic, and humanistic attacks on the Scripture. We also combat the so-called 'Modernistic,' 'Liberal,' and 'Neo-Orthodox' positions. . . . Every teacher in the University signs our orthodox creed once a year" (9).[46] Bob Jones University, like most other conservative Christian universities and colleges, warns prospective students that their attendance is a privilege and that the university retains its right to dismiss them for improper faith as well as conduct. James Davison Hunter points out that these institutional articles of faith are consonant with the central task of fundamentalism in this country since the nineteenth century—the marking of its boundaries. The object is to attain doctrinal *and* social integrity. "Such criteria," Hunter explains, "provide a test for group membership: those who adhere belong; those who do not adhere entirely or on particular points do not belong. While all ideological systems . . . maintain cognitive, moral, and behavioral boundaries of one sort or another, religious orthodoxies are often distinguished by the narrowness with which these lines are drawn and the strictness with which they are enforced" (19–20). As the Bob Jones University bulletin reveals, the criteria which demarcate these theological and social boundaries provide a necessary but not sufficient power. An institution must also have the right to dismiss those who, if they remain within, would change the orthodoxy.[47]

Fundamentalists are taking over conservative Christian colleges, universities, and seminaries where they intend to employ doctrinally correct faculty to teach doctrinally correct students. But what will they teach these students to do? Nicholas Wolterstorff identifies three models for conservative Christian institutions: the Christian humanist model that initiates "the student into the Christian mind"; the Christian academic-discipline model that introduces the student "to the disciplines as developed and conducted in fidelity to the Christian gospel"; and the Christian socialization model that trains the student to carry out the Christian calling in his occupation or profession.[48] Certainly the first two goals are embraced by all the institutions, but the largest programs at those controlled or influenced by fundamentalists train students in mass media, church administration, Christian theology, education, and social work. In view of the huge churches, the big business of fundraising, the proliferation of evangelical media, and the expanding system of Christian education, these programs are intended to train the first generation of *professional* fundamentalists, that is, professionals whose business is the advancement of fundamentalism. Reflecting, as well as enabling, the movement toward professionalization, the bulletins of these institutions employ the discourse of liberal higher education. Courses on how to build fundamentalist churches, conduct world missions, lead Christian communities, and use the media to evangelize are described as "surveys" or "seminars," have "course designators" and "credits," require "research" or "practicum," and emphasize "techniques" and "analysis." The obvious reason these institutions use this discourse is that to receive student aid and accreditation, as most of them do, they must satisfy the requirements of professional associations and licensing boards. But there is another, more frightening reason for their recent professionalism. It masks the fact that fundamentalists have transformed the traditional goals of liberal higher education (to cultivate the faculties of individuals and to produce knowledge) into the goal of instrumental education (to develop the expertise they need to evangelize America).[49]

The course offerings listed in institutional bulletins attest to this goal. For instance, Southeastern Baptist Theological Seminary in Wake Forest, North Carolina, offers:

H2240 CHURCH GROWTH AND MISSIONARY STRATEGIES. An analytical study of the Church Growth approach to missionary strategy, especially the principles of church multiplication, people movements, homogeneous units, and the statistical measuring of Christian growth.
T3323 THE CHURCH AND SOCIAL CHANGE. A study of selected ecumenical, denominational, and church models for social change with special attention to the church's social strategy and the theological justification for programs of social reform.

Social change, the aim of these courses, is itself the subject of another course, titled "M4626 CHRISTIAN LEADERSHIP AND CHANGE MANAGEMENT."

The boldest program at these universities, and surprisingly at many seminaries as well, is mass media. Liberty University offers some thirty-two courses in church management, but at least forty in radio and television. Bob Jones University offers nineteen courses in church management, but forty in radio and television and another twenty-four in cinema. All of these courses, technical and creative, are intended to be instrumental. For instance, Oral Roberts University's "CHRM 431. MASS MEDIA EVANGELISM" is "A study of the nature of evangelism and of mass media. Strategies for using mass media for world evangelism." Southern Baptist Theological Seminary in Louisville, Kentucky, offers:

3110. MASS MEDIA AND CHRISTIAN MESSAGE. An examination of the roles and influences of mass media in contemporary culture and options for utilizing mass media in the redemptive work of the church. Emphases will be placed on practical production experience.
3120. CREATIVE USE OF RADIO AND TELEVISION IN THE LOCAL CHURCH. An examination of programming for the mass media, including investigations of current programming trends, models of religious broadcasting, and creative approaches toward using the media to communicate Christian messages.
3268. STRATEGIES FOR MEDIA EVANGELISM. An investigation of factors involved in planning and activating a strategy for using the mass media in communicating the Christian message in a local area. Emphasis will be placed on audience analysis, marketing techniques, media forums, and feedback tools.

Like the traditional courses in aviation, which taught missionaries how to reach the homelands of prospective converts, and in preaching, which taught them how to touch their hearts, the new courses in mass media teach professional evangelists how to enter our systems of cultural production and use them to Christianize us.

Next Moves

In "Feminism and the Politics of Education," Mary O'Brien remarks that "the notion of education as an objective uncovering of truth and a subjective passing on of knowledge obscures the fact that truth and knowledge are socially defined and legitimated and that the power to define meanings and identify what is to be 'acceptable truth' is a very real power, exercised day by day in the bureaucracies and classrooms of educational systems everywhere" (91). The social construction of knowledge, the use of education to construct reality, and the complete implication of power in these endeavors are what feminists have confronted in their critiques of liberal education and their development of women's studies. In these respects, as well as in their indictments of liberal hegemony, the New Right and feminism are similar. Both groups want to use education to make social change. "This," O'Brien explains, "is why feminism has been a major sociohistorical determinant of the extremist politics of neo-conservatism: New Right organizers understand better than professional politicians the implications of feminist curricular innovation for family stability and ideological hegemony" (92). Diverse as their own constituencies are, the right, middle, and left are now more dramatically triangulated than they have been in the past. Their ideologies of human nature, society, and authority, as well as their cultural strategies, place them antithetically. What next?

I return now to the question I asked earlier: How likely is the New Right to succeed in implementing its dogmatic and oppressive version of a Christian America? My answer is a stark one. The New Right aims to control education because it is a crucial instrument in creating a Christian America. It is moving strategically in two directions: while eroding our system of higher education, it is building its own system of Christian colleges, universities, and seminaries to train the professionals who will perform this work. Will the Right succeed? Will feminism? Comparatively speaking, these are our strategic resources:

1. Churches are the infrastructure for local political efforts of the Christian Right. These efforts are substantial ones when they are made by Jerry Falwell's Thomas Road Baptist Church in Virginia with 21,000 members and

$75.5 million annual income or by Greg Dixon's smaller 8,000-member Indianapolis Baptist Temple.[50] Local feminist organizations, like chapters of NOW or NARAL, count their members in the hundreds.

2. The mailing lists assembled by Richard Viguerie and used for New Right fundraising and organizing contain more than twenty-five million names. Feminists have no comparable mailing lists.

3. Today, the Christian Right has some 470 television stations and 1,300 radio stations that reach an estimated audience of ten to forty million people weekly and raise contributions of $6 billion annually.[51] Feminists have no television or radio stations and have made virtually no impact on commercial or public ones.

4. In 1985, the Christian Right had over 300 periodicals, which were increasing at the rate of twenty to twenty-five per year, 70 publishing houses, an Evangelical Press Association, and 6,000 Christian bookstores. Feminists had as many periodicals, a dozen feminist presses, and feminist bookstores in several cities and towns.[52]

5. The Christian Right has built an educational system of 17,000 schools and 250 colleges, universities, and seminaries. Feminists have built 500 women's studies programs in colleges and universities. While feminists are trying to transform traditional curricula, conservatives are trying to erode the institutions that house these curricula.[53]

I have focused on strategy because I believe that in contests of this sort the question of who prevails is not necessarily decided by moral and intellectual merit, as liberal ideology would have us believe, but by power to produce the intended results. In producing the intended results, the New Right has been far more effective than liberals, feminists, or leftists.

Readers who take this appraisal of strategy as seriously as I do must be wondering what recommendations I shall make. Because I am unwilling to make detailed recommendations where the New Right has easy access to them, I can make only a few recommendations here. First, we must make *strategic* moves. Ideologically, feminists may have improved upon the liberating ideas of the Left in the early 1970s, but strategically we have not matched the New Right's success in making change where the Left failed. Second, we need to begin (one can hardly say continue) the hard work of transforming liberal individualism as a system of thought and life. Liberal individualism is ideologically and strategically bankrupt, and only its historically attained ownership of the institutions and resources of this country has postponed the disintegration that the New Right is trying to precipitate. Third, we need to form a new coalition that includes constituencies from the left, center, and right. To do this coalition-building, we will have to learn how to talk to conservative women, moderate evangelicals, and liberal Catholics and Mormons.

Most important, we need to hold a national retreat that will allow representative educators—faculty, administrators, foundation directors, agents for change, experts on the New Right, and feminists—to begin doing the action-planning for higher education that we should have been doing since 1979.

Meanwhile, I want to conclude, as I began, with an anecdote. Three years ago in Cincinnati, where I used to live, the New Right sent national activists to stir up the town. They held a concert, and the next morning they bombed the Planned Parenthood Clinic. A community of women, civic leaders, educators, and clergy joined together one evening to protest this violence. At the rally, the Rev. Maurice McCracken, an octogenarian social rights activist, spoke. The words with which he ended his speech on that evening I borrow to end mine now: "In times such as these," he said—and I add so that we all know what is at stake, in times when the definition of human beings, the forces for social order, and all the ideas we teach are up for grabs— "in times such as these," he said, "there are no innocent bystanders. If you're a bystander, you're not innocent." Knowing what we know now, the wrong move would be not to move.

Notes

I wish to thank the Graduate School of the University of Minnesota for a Grant-in-Aid of Research during 1986–87; Judith Halberstam, Graduate Research Assistant, and Patricia D. Stark, Education Librarian, Walter Library, for their helpful research; and Betty Jean Craige, Arthur Geffen, Michael Hancher, and Joan E. Hartman for their comments on an earlier version of this essay. I dedicate this essay to Warren Bennis, Joseph DeBell Professor of Management and Organization, University of Southern California, in appreciation of his work as a university president and his writings on higher education.

1 Tim LaHaye, *The Battle for the Mind* (Old Tappan, N.J.: Fleming H. Revell, 1980), p. 25. LaHaye has oversimplified the view of conservative Christian scholars that the history of higher education from medieval times to the present is a history of Christian education successively eroded by Renaissance humanism, Enlightenment skepticism, revolutionary philosophy, the nineteenth-century secularization of American colleges and universities, and the twentieth-century monopoly of liberal humanism. For histories of Christian higher education, see the first seven essays in *Making Higher Education Christian: The History and Mission of Evangelical Colleges in America,* ed. Joel A. Carpenter and Kenneth W. Shipps (Grand Rapids, Mich.: Christian University Press/Eerdmans, 1987); and William C. Ringenberg, *The Christian College: A History of Protestant Higher Education in America* (Grand Rapids, Mich.: Eerdmans, 1984).
2 Jerome L. Himmelstein, "The New Right," in *The New Christian Right: Mobiliza-*

tion and Legitimation, ed. Robert Liebman and Robert Wuthnow (New York: Aldine, 1983), p. 24.

3 Ben Brodinsky, "The New Right: The Movement and Its Impact," *Phi Delta Kappan* (October 1982): 88.

4 See Himmelstein, pp. 13–15; and Brodinsky, p. 88.

5 Besides *The New Christian Right,* see James Davison Hunter, *American Evangelicalism: Conservative Religion and the Quandary of Modernity* (New Brunswick: Rutgers University Press, 1983); and Mary O'Brien, "Feminism and the Politics of Education," *Interchange* 17.2 (Summer 1986): 93.

6 President Ronald Reagan perfectly restated the conservative idea of the integration of society and religion in his speech to the Ecumenical Prayer Breakfast at the Republican National Convention in Dallas, Texas, on August 23, 1984: "The truth is, politics and morality are inseparable. And as morality's foundation is religion, religion and politics are necessarily related. We need religion as a guide. We need it because we are imperfect. And our government needs the church because only those humble enough to admit they're sinners can bring to democracy the tolerance it requires in order to survive" (reported in the *New York Times,* 24 August 1984, A1, A11). For a full discussion of evangelical ideology, see Hunter, note 5.

7 See James L. Guth, "The New Christian Right," in *The New Christian Right,* p. 33; and Robert C. Liebman, "Mobilizing the Moral Majority," ibid., p. 53.

8 Quoted in introduction to *The New Christian Right,* pp. 6–7.

9 "TV's Unholy Row," *Time,* 6 April 1987, 60, 63; "God and Money," *Newsweek,* 6 April 1987, 20.

10 Jerry Falwell, *Listen, America* (Garden City, N.Y.: Doubleday, 1980), p. xi.

11 His charges are no more extreme and his rhetoric no less shrill than those of other conservatives. Here, for instance, is the opening of Carl Sommer's feature story titled "Education: Schools in Crisis":

> Two ideologies in today's education conflict. One advocates permissiveness, freedom without responsibility, profane textbooks, parental disrespect, laxity toward misbehavior, situational ethics, maximum individual autonomy, sexual license, euthanasia, right to suicide, anti-Americanism, and atheism.
>
> The other favors discipline, law and order, freedom with responsibility, work ethic, academic excellence, parental respect, decent textbooks, sexual purity, patriotism, and theism.
>
> The conflict is between humanism and the traditional American value system based upon a theistic ethic. Once this humanistic philosophy is understood, it becomes clear that its progressive teaching has permeated not only our schools but our society, and it continues to be the archenemy of educational success and national morality (*Moral Majority Report* [September 1985]: 4; also see Carl Sommer, *Schools in Crisis: Training for Success or Failure* [Houston: Cahill, 1984]).

12 James Davison Hunter, *Evangelism: The Coming Generation* (Chicago: University of Chicago Press, 1987), p. 6. For a fine account of education in such a school, see Alan Peshkin, *God's Choice: The Total World of a Fundamentalist Christian School* (Chicago: University of Chicago Press, 1986).

13 *Reader's Digest 1987 Almanac* (Pleasantville, N.Y.: Reader's Digest, 1987), pp. 206–47.

14 See Ringenberg's *The Christian College* (pp. 147–214) for an account of the Christian responses to the secularization of higher education—the development of Bible colleges, liberal arts colleges, universities, and seminaries, supported by government aid, work-study arrangements, and televangelist fundraising.

15 Personal communication from an anonymous source, December 1979.

16 Margaret Ann Latus, "Ideological PACS and Political Action," in *The New Christian Right,* p. 89 ff.

17 Donald Heinz, "The Struggle to Define America," in *The New Christian Right,* p. 134. Also see Eileen M. Gardiner, "The Growth of the Federal Role in Education," *A New Agenda for Education,* ed. Eileen M. Gardner, Critical Issues Series (Washington, D.C.: Heritage Foundation, 1985), pp. 27–46; and Philip F. Lawler, "Higher Education Today," ibid., pp. 47–58, for a conservative analysis of the federal control of higher education through funding policies and practices.

18 The decision in *Grove City College* attempted to limit the federal regulation that could occur when students accepted government-subsidized loans to the unit(s) directly subsidized by the loans—for instance, the division of student aid but not the history department or the athletic program.

19 The story that President Reagan told in his speech to the Ecumenical Prayer Breakfast is the familiar conservative Christian one about a nation founded in Christianity and eroded by a "secularization movement" that during the 1960s took religion out of the schools and other public institutions. See the reprint of his speech in the *New York Times,* 24 August 1984, A11. This speech is quoted extensively in Jerry Falwell's *Moral Majority National Issues Survey,* a direct-mail brochure distributed in February 1985. Polling the recipients on ten matters of concern to the Christian Right, Falwell promises: "You will have a direct impact on President Reagan's agenda for the next four years. That's because Jerry Falwell will inform the President of the views of you and your fellow Americans when he meets with him on his regular visits to the White House."

The American Studies Program, sponsored by the conservative Christian College Coalition, is another example of the integration of religion and politics. The Coalition says that "because of its unique location in the nation's capital, the ASP is viewed as a special way of challenging students to consider the meaning of proclaiming the Lordship of Jesus Christ in all areas of life, including career choices, public policy issues and personal relations. During the fall and spring terms, students . . . are engaged in two principal activities: working as unpaid interns in their intended vocational fields and studying public policy issues in seminar classes. The internships have placed numerous students in Congressional offices, Executive agencies, legal offices, lobbying and research groups, social service agencies, cultural institutions, and other businesses throughout Washington" (*A Guide to Christian Colleges* [Grand Rapids: Eerdmans, 1982], p. 129).

20 Fred L. Pincus, "From Equity to Excellence: The Rebirth of Educational Conservatism," *Social Policy* 14.3 (Winter 1984): 51.

21 Terrel H. Bell, "Education Policy Development in the Reagan Administration," *Phi Delta Kappan* 67.7 (March 1986): 488.

22 For an account that aligns Bell more closely with the radical Right agenda, see David L. Clark and Mary Ann Amiot, "The Disassembly of the Federal Educational Role," *Education and Urban Society* 15.3 (May 1983): 367–87.

23 Robert Scholes, "Aiming a Canon at the Curriculum," *Salmagundi* 72 (Fall 1986): 102.

24 E. D. Hirsch, Jr., " 'Cultural Literacy' Does Not Mean 'Canon,' " *Salmagundi* 72 (Fall 1986): 120.

25 E. D. Hirsch, Jr., Joseph Kett, and James Trefil, "Appendix: What Literate Americans Know: A Preliminary List," in E. D. Hirsch, Jr., *Cultural Literacy* (Boston: Houghton Mifflin, 1987), pp. 146–215.

26 "A New Agenda for Education," in *A New Agenda for Education*, p. 79.

27 Nathan O. Hatch, "Evangelical Colleges and the Challenge of Christian Thinking," in *Making Higher Education Christian*, p. 158.

28 William J. Bennett, "The Shattered Humanities," *Wall Street Journal*, 31 December 1982, p. 10. Bennett's terminology—shattered, relative liberal knowledge and integrated, authoritative conservative knowledge—comes from the discourse of conservative Christian scholars and educators. See William C. Ringenberg, *The Christian College;* Nathan O. Hatch, "Evangelical Colleges and the Challenge of Christian Thinking," in *Making Higher Education Christian;* and a book to which these authors are indebted, Arthur F. Holmes, *The Idea of a Christian College*, rev. ed. (Grand Rapids, Mich.: Eerdmans, 1975).

29 "To Reclaim a Legacy," printed in *Chronicle of Higher Education*, 28 November 1984, 16. The rhetoric that Bennett employs in this report of inheritance, tradition, and authority is the rhetoric of property that Edmund Burke used so effectively in his great conservative polemic, *Reflections on the Revolution in France*, and more recently the rhetoric of cultural inheritance used by conservative educators (*e.g.*, E. D. Hirsch, Jr.; and Nicholas Wolterstorff, "Teaching for Justice," in *Making Higher Education Christian*, p. 205).

30 "Education Dept. Sets Fewer Trips for Civil-Rights Officials, More for Bennett," *Chronicle of Higher Education*, 7 May 1986, 13, 14.

31 Robin Wilson, "A Finely Tuned Public-Relations Effort Keeps Bennett in the Public Eye," *Chronicle of Higher Education*, 10 December 1986, 16.

32 Stacey E. Palmer, "Bennett's Plans Would Ruin Innovative Fund, Congress Told," *Chronicle of Higher Education*, 18 September 1985, 15.

33 "Bennett Fires Chief of Popular Agency, Picks Close Advisor as Replacement," *Chronicle of Higher Education*, 28 October 1986, 19.

34 In an apparently less controversial use of federal funds, NEH has supported the Christian College Coalition's workshops designed to investigate a theoretical basis for conservative Christian higher education. See *Making Higher Education Christian*, p. 149. I cannot help wondering why the use of NEH funds to develop conservative Christian theory but the restriction of NEH funds from ideological (meaning feminist and Marxist) projects goes unremarked.

35 According to the feminist critique, educational and other social institutions are manufacturing consent to live in patriarchy. Fundamentalists and feminists criticize schools, families, and workplaces on the same grounds—their production of an unwanted ideology—and propose that these institutions produce their ideology. We differ in our ideologies and the strategies for implementing them. Alan Peshkin's *God's Choice: The Total World of a Fundamentalist Christian School* shows how fundamentalists use a school to manufacture consent to live in Christianity.

36 Annette Kirk and Russell Kirk, "The Demise of the Teaching Profession," in *A New Agenda for Education,* p. 1.

37 Magali Sarfatti Larson, *The Rise of Professionalism: A Sociological Analysis* (Berkeley: University of California Press, 1977), p. xiii.

38 See Thomas A. Askew, "The Shaping of Evangelical Higher Education Since World War II," in *Making Higher Education Christian*, pp. 137–52. He believes that conservative Christian institutions are entering a third phase of development, which he calls "Professionalization, Networks, and Theoretical Understanding."

39 "Text of Secretary Bennett's Speech on College Costs and U.S. Student Aid," *Chronicle of Higher Education*, 26 November 1986, 21. Also see Jean Evangelauf, "Bennett Castigates Colleges over Skyrocketing Tuition, Proposes Changes in U.S. Student Aid to Control Costs," *ibid.*, 1, 21.

40 Rebecca B. Rubin, Marie A. Whaley, Nancy E. Mitchell, and Karen Sharp, "Affirmative Action on Campus," *Academe* 70.5 (November–December 1984): 27.

41 All information on costs and enrollments is from *The College Blue Book: Tabular Data* (New York: MacMillan, 1987).

42 "After Election Win, Baptist Fundamentalists Seen Certain to Gain Control of Seminaries," *Chronicle of Higher Education*, 18 June 1986, 24. Also see David McKenzie, "Teaching Students Who Already Know the 'Truth,' " *Thought & Action: The NEA Higher Education Journal* 2.1 (Winter 1986): 112–14.

43 On Southeastern, see "Southeastern Baptist College Leaders Vow to Fight 'Takeover' as Fundamentalists Seek Control of Governing Boards," *Chronicle of Higher Education*, 21 October 1987, 15–16; and "President and Dean Quit Baptist Seminary Posts in Protest over Fundamentalists' Interference," *Chronicle of Higher Education*, 4 November 1987, 19–20. On Mercer, also see Barbara Kantrowitz and Andrew Murr, "Going Topless and Other Sins," *Newsweek*, 26 October 1987, 80.

44 "Baptists' Leaders Defend Drive to Make Seminaries Reflect Fundamentalism," *Chronicle of Higher Education*, 25 June 1986, 3.

45 *A Guide to Christian Colleges* (Grand Rapids: Eerdmans/Christian College Coalition, 1982), p. 118. Advancing the centrality of conservative religious ideology to education, the Christian College Coalition recently "commissioned a number of these scholars [conservative Christian scholars trained in secular research universities] to produce a series of supplemental textbooks to provide Christian perspectives on the major academic disciplines" (Timothy L. Sweet, "Introduction: Christian Colleges and American Culture," in *Making Higher Education Christian*, p. 6).

46 Here and elsewhere I refer to the 1986–87 bulletins of the following institutions: Southern Baptist Theological Seminary, Louisville, Ky.; Midwestern Baptist Theological Seminary, Kansas City, Mo.; Southeastern Baptist Theological Seminary, Wake Forest, N.C.; Golden Gate Baptist Theological Seminary, Mill Valley, Calif.; Liberty University (formerly Liberty Baptist College), Lynchburg, Va.; Mercer University, Macon, Ga.; Wake Forest University, Winston-Salem, N.C.; Oral Roberts University, Tulsa, Okla.; Bob Jones University, Greenville, S.C.; Furman University, Greenville, N.C.; Mars Hill College, Mars Hill, N.C.; Bethel College, Mishawaka, Ind.; Christian Heritage College, El Cajon, Calif. I have also read an institutional self-study produced by Bethel College in anticipation of its accreditation review.

47 Nathan O. Hatch, a conservative Christian scholar, also acknowledges that the marking of boundaries to insure doctrinal and social integrity is an important issue in the development of Christian higher education. See "Evangelical Colleges and the Challenge of Christian Thinking," in *Making Higher Education Christian,* p. 161.

48 Nicholas Wolterstorff, "Teaching for Justice," in *Making Higher Education Christian,* pp. 206, 208.

49 For a statement about the instrumentalism of conservatives in using education to procure material, rather than religious, ends, see Peter Augustine Lawler, "Reaganism, Liberal Education, and Conservatism," *College Teaching* 34.3 (Summer 1986): 105.

50 See "TV's Unholy Row," 60–63; "God and Money," 18–20; and Liebman, 58–59.

51 Donald Heinz, "The Struggle to Define America," in *The New Christian Right,* p. 139; "TV's Unholy Row" and "God and Money," cited above.

52 See Hunter, p. 7; *Women in Print II: Opportunities for Women's Studies Publication in Language and Literature,* ed. Joan E. Hartman and Ellen Messer-Davidow (New York: Modern Language Association, 1982); and Polly Joan and Andrea Chesman, *Guide to Women's Publishing* (Paradise, Calif.: Dustbooks, 1978). The Christian University Press, a subsidiary of the Christian College Consortium, and William B. Eerdmans Publishing Company are frequent publishers of conservative Christian scholarship; and the Bob Jones University Press is reportedly publishing a series of high school textbooks (Peshkin 115).

53 For data on schools, see Hunter, p. 6. For a listing of colleges, universities, and seminaries with affiliations, see *Reader's Digest 1987 Almanac.* For a listing of women's studies programs, see *PMLA* 102.4 (September 1987): 640–47.

Politics and Academic Research

Catharine R. Stimpson

In May 1986, I chaired a meeting of the New York Council for the Humanities, which organizes and funds projects for the public in the humanities. One of our decisions was to award $10,000 to underwrite completion costs and public screenings for a documentary that filmmakers had prepared with three humanities scholars. The camera and academic research were conjoined. The film, "Cuba: In the Shadow of Doubt," was a history of the Cuban revolution and of Fidel Castro's huge part in that process.

In October 1986, a conservative group called Accuracy in Media, Inc. (AIM) went after "Cuba: In the Shadow of Doubt."[1] At best, AIM asserted, we were apologists for "monster" Castro and for monstrous Communism. The unvarnished truth about Castro was in *Against All Hope*, Armando Valladares's narrative about the twenty-two years he spent in prison in Cuba. AIM urged its readers to write to the film's financial backers and denounce their decision.

I prepared a brief statement that defended the film, the diversity of its perspectives, and the solidity of its historical narrative to mail out in response to the denunciations that did tumble in. In mid-November, I received an especially chilling letter from a consulting engineer in Baton Rouge, Louisiana. He told me that my statement was "totally unsatisfactory." He then imagined that I was a documentary filmmaker in Nazi Germany. In his somewhat incoherent fantasy, I would: "make sure that Goebbels was given a chance to show . . . Germany's better side and then have someone give . . . a phrase or two on the fine concentration camps." After another flurry in which the correspondent compared me to Adolph Eichmann, he assured me that he did not approve of censorship. I could waste my own money in any way I liked.

However, I could not shell out his tax dollars on "procommunist material."

Obviously, my anecdote is a parable about contemporary politics and academic research. The police of the New Right are vigilantly patrolling academic precincts. They are especially concerned with scholarship that reaches a large audience through public libraries, films, television, and textbooks. Their language may be florid, lurid, and garish, but their organization is taut and skillful. Perhaps less obviously, my anecdote is also an anti-parable, in that it illustrates a tempting way of representing reality that we must resist. This way is to reduce the world to a polarized set of binary oppositions. The engineer sees but two parties: the party of God, freedom-loving American patriots, and the party of the devil, prison-building Communists and their fellow travelers. He thinks only of the red-white-and-blue and the red. I, in turn, could see but two parties as well: the party of civilized liberal thought and the party of the loony, repressive right wing.

In 1987, however, the relationships between politics and academic research are too intricate, their mutually entangled lines of force too numerous and pulsating, to permit binary oppositions to name and order them. Moreover, neither the New Right nor the New Left is monolithic. Elements in the New Right, for example, might share a commitment to less governmental regulation of the economy and greater laissez-faire for the marketplace, lower taxes, an end to the minimum wage, the replacement of welfare by workfare, a fervent anti-Communism and a strong defense, and the "traditional" family and parental control of education. These same elements might split apart, however, on the nature of biblical authority or the practice of libertarianism.

Let me mention four sources of complexity:

1) The sheer number and variety of places that sponsor research and endorse researchers. The United States has libraries; museums; about 3,000 institutions of higher education, each with its own roster of faculty members and network of departments; disciplinary organizations, each with its own rules of advancement; and over 9,700 university-related and other nonprofit research organizations.[2] No single ideological agenda can inspire them all. This mass hampers too tidy and confident a correlation between a particular administration and a particular kind of research. One might have expected more research about minorities in American Studies in the 1970s than in the 1980s, since federal policies in this current decade have been so hostile to civil rights and education equity. Yet, at the 1987 American Studies Association meeting, Professor Richard A. Yarborough reported that articles in *American Quarterly,* the journal of that organization, peaked between 1964 and 1973, declined in the 1970s, and rose again in 1983.[3]

2) The number of funding sources for research. In 1986, fifteen federal agencies obligated $6,538,280,000 for research and development to colleges

and universities. Joining them were regional, state, and local governments and private sources, especially foundations. Humanists sadly know, in our budgets and bare bones, how little research money we receive in comparison to those in the sciences, medicine, and engineering. The economic marginality of the humanities is probably more dangerous than the frightened, hostile attacks on "secular humanism" by the New Right. In the late 1980s, the most compelling research trends seem to leave the humanities out. Instead, these trends push toward computerization and university-industry cooperation for the sake of economic development, be it national, regional, state, or local. "Technology transfers" have become a fetish.[4]

To be sure, the 1970s were the site for the development of wealthy foundations (for example, the Sarah Scaife, Adolph Coors, Samuel Roberts Noble, or John M. Olin) that lavishly financed conservative causes and research. In 1985, the Sarah Scaife Foundation gave $200,000 for a public TV film on religion in "Russia"; $150,000 to the *New Criterion;* and $25,000 to the Institute for Humane Studies in Fairfax, Virginia. It also contributed $107,000 to the Carnegie Institution for acquisitions and $250,000 to the National Gallery of Art. Despite their strength, which I do not underestimate, these foundations do not have enough power to control research. The 1985 Sarah Scaife grants were five out of 5,998 grants with a total value of $279,408,960 from 378 foundations in support of arts and culture.[5]

Support for research about women and girls serves as a case study for the inability of a single political agenda to control America's multiple bankrolls. In 1985 and early 1986, 320 foundations gave a total of $75,562,742 in 2,160 grants of $5,000 or more to support projects for women and girls.[6] The Ford Foundation was the leader, giving $11,397,965 in 134 separate grants, three times more than the next most generous foundations, Robert Wood Johnson and Rockefeller. Of the comparatively paltry sum of $75,562,742, 15.4 percent went to higher education; 0.9 percent to adult or continuing education; a little over 11 percent to the social sciences and humanities. Some, but by no means all, of these grants were for academic research (for example, cataloging the Emma Goldman papers).

Apparently, only a few grants were for clearly right-wing organizations: the Richardson Foundation gave $35,000 to the Committee for the Free World for a project called "Women and Families for Defense"; the ubiquitous Olin Foundation gave $25,000 to the Eagle Forum Education and Legal Defense Fund for "educational" programs on comparable worth. The number of grants may be low partly because the New Right resists making "women" a separate category of analysis and, therefore, of funding but also because much foundation funding goes to various points on the spectrum of the political and social middle. It flows through the river channels cut midway between the opposing cliffs and banks of more radical beliefs. Many grants went to sound, ongoing institutions: Girls' Clubs, the Girl Scouts, schools and colleges, scholarship programs. I could discern only a few grants to racially marked women's causes: just twenty-six were indexed under "black women." Nor could I tease out much *explicit* feminism: only twenty-two grants went to women's studies, as such, in the United States and abroad; only a few recipients had feminist names, usually the Feminist Press; only four grants explicitly used the word *lesbian*. All from the Chicago Resource Center, these four went for support of a gay and lesbian film festival, a project on violence in lesbian relationships, a study of black lesbian relationships, and general help for lesbian programs in a women's coalition.

Feminism was in place, however, titularly erased though it might be. Project after project was devoted to a feminist cause: poor and minority women; prenatal care; health; teenage pregnancy; self-empowerment through employment; and, frequently, the treatment and prevention of rape and domestic violence. The presence of a cause, but not of its name, may be the consequence of strategic thinking on the part of proposal writers. With some reason, they have concluded that people respond positively to the goals of feminism, but negatively to the word. More important, since the 1960s the language of feminism, if not the word itself, has sufficiently influenced United States discourse to become a familiar, unremarkable element of that discourse.

To a lesser degree, the feminist shaping of advanced thinking appears in federal research funding from the National Endowment for the Humanities. The grants collated in the endowment's 1986 annual report vividly show the desire of the Reagan Administration to conserve and restock an ideal of Western culture. Of the thirty-five exemplary projects in undergraduate and graduate education, five use the charged signifiers *masterpiece* or *classic* or *central* in their titles. Three are devoted to canonical authors. Another category, grants to "Foster Coherence Throughout An Institution," shows support of $1,490,933 to thirteen disparate institutions for the purpose of promoting a core curriculum and "great texts." Four of those thirty-five exemplary projects, however, seem to concern the new scholarship about women—too many to be tokenism, though too few to be muscular. An equivalent weighting occurs in the fellowship awards: 147 went to university teachers in Ph.D.-granting institutions and 110 to independent scholars and teachers in non-Ph.D.-granting institutions. A project title can be opaque. What will Jonathan Arac do with "American Prose Narrative, 1830s through 1860s"? Nevertheless, of the 147 grants, I counted several individual projects on peasants or the working classes and perhaps eleven on women and/or minorities. One went to Annette Kolodny for a study of feminist criticism. Twenty-one or twenty-two were for studies of canonical figures, the number depending on whom one elevates into the canon. Suggestively, of the 110 fellowships for college teachers and for independent scholars, eighteen had women and/or minorities as their subject and fifteen had canonical figures. In brief, the more prestigious the institution (according to standard criteria, such as granting a highly reputable Ph.D.), the more male fellowship winners and the more conventional the subject matter. Thirty women were among the university faculty. (I excluded a Helen C. White Hall of Madison, Wisconsin, with a project on "Reality and the Forms of Narrative in American Fiction, 1945–72"). Forty-six women were among the college teachers and independent scholars. Such figures are less guides to the New Right than to the class structure of academic institutions.

3) The ferocity of the struggles for resources, because they are there, and between personalities and egos, because *they* are there. Even though such battles are symptomatic of a masculinized American culture of research that values competitiveness, they also take on a half-life of their own. Randy Shilts's *And The Band Played On: Politics, People, and the AIDS Epidemic* is a horrifying account of the connections between politics and academic research.[7] Shilts shows heroes in action: some doctors and nurses; some scientists who believe that caring for the sick is a responsibility that transcends any political program; some politicians; the dying AIDS victims and their families. Bitterly, however, he demonstrates what delayed the search for the cause of AIDS and transmogrified AIDS into an epidemic more devastating than it needed to become: vicious, but commonplace homophobia; Reagan budget policies and public relations; the discourse and administration of big science; the ways in which the media select their stories; the internal politics of the gay movement; and finally, the rampaging egos of researchers, among them Robert Gallo of the National Cancer Institute.

4) The pervasive, lingering power of a language that represents research as objective, politically uncontaminated and innocent, and value free. The *Twenty-First Annual Report of the National Endowment for the Humanities* (1986) has an ostensibly no-nonsense, but actually pious, message from the deputy chairman: "We are firm in the belief that an agency supported by public funds may not use any portion of its money to fund partisan, ideological, or political positions. . . . [T]his agency will resist funding projects that use the humanities to promote any particular social agenda. . . . [T]hose projects that legitimately wish to examine issues of current controversy must do so in a balanced manner."[8] Manipulating such a language, the self-descriptions of research centers and foundations in various directories are bland. Their categories of activity are merely nouns, subjects without predicates, deeds aloof from committed movements. The term "public interest" covers grants that, to the uninitiated observer, might as easily support as oppose Star Wars. What is the

Christianity Today Institute in Carol Stream, Illinois, doing under the leadership of its executive director, Terry Muck, as it conducts research into the evangelical Christian community, aging, minorities, feminism, humanism, and the secularization of America?

Refreshingly, a few groups are more direct. Paralleling modern and postmodern critiques of "objectivity," they announce politically charged intentions through an easily broken code or plain talk. In the *Research Center Directory,* in 1988, the John M. Ashbrook Center for Public Affairs, at Ashland College, Ohio, declares that its research activity is "development of the conservative philosophy in the twentieth and twenty-first centuries." In a profile, the Ford Foundation speaks of its concern for the "welfare of the rural poor," or "the quality of education available to members of disadvantaged groups."[9] If the word *freedom* gives conservatives a rallying cry and marker of political faith, *equality* is just as gratifying for liberals.

In American higher education, an institutional counterpoint to the belief in objectivity and value-free research is the commitment to academic freedom. This is the often smarmy, self-congratulatory, and holey rubric under which scholarship defends itself from overtly political intrusions and permits professors to make unpopular statements. Nevertheless, "academic freedom," like the theory of value-free research, helps to legitimize an invaluable intellectual space in which a single perspective or polemic cannot run rampant. The disputatious genre, polemic deliberately uses language like a poleax. It puts ire into irenics. At its most destructive, polemical speech resembles the diatribe of the neurotic. One vision of the world, which trauma and pain have shaped, irrevocably, univocally, becomes the world. In a sense, academic freedom encourages the holders of various perspectives and polemics to enter into a treaty that offers a mild, scholarly version of the defense strategy of mutually assured destruction: "If you hurt me by making me think like you, I'll hurt you by making you think like me."

The first American definitions of academic freedom were the work of thirteen professors rather than of lawyers, although Roscoe Pound of the Harvard Law School was among the thirteen. In 1915, the organizational meeting of the American Association of University Professors created a Committee on Academic Freedom and Academic Tenure. Its famous 1915 "Declaration of Principles" is the Ur-document of modern academic freedom. The declaration argued that academic freedom—that combination of privilege, right, necessity, and responsibility—consisted of three elements: "freedom of inquiry and research; freedom of teaching within the university or college; and freedom of extra-mural utterance and action."[10] To be sure, the declaration said that academic freedom would not apply to all institutions. There were, for example, proprietary institutions in which a founder might have left his estate for the teaching of a specific doctrine. However, the declaration explicitly stated that most educational institutions, public or private, operate for the public good and as a public trust. As a result, such institutions must embody an academic freedom that operates for the public good. Indeed, one of the most persistent, influential features of the 1915 declaration is the crucial belief that academic freedom is not an entitlement for a few remote scholars but a public good.

Sustaining that belief has been a taut political and cultural logic, which postmodern inquiry is now anatomizing without displacing the authority of the concept of academic freedom itself: 1) A democracy needs intellectual ferment and enlightened opinions; 2) However, these goods cannot exist without freedom of inquiry, disinterestedness, impartiality, and the unimpeded exchange of ideas; 3) Because the basis of a scholar's academic freedom is the public good, he (the generic *he* haunts early writings about academic freedom), in turn, must behave in a publicly responsible way. Even when he speaks as a private citizen, he ought to show the ideal (some might say "idealized") characteristics of his profession: accuracy, restraint, and a decent respect for the opinions of others. The power of this belief, and of its sustaining logic, appears, for example, in the 1940 "Statement of Principles of Academic Freedom and Tenure," which the AAUP and the Association of American Colleges issued. Since 1940, over one hundred disciplinary societies have endorsed this statement. Its provisions have been incorporated into the bylaws of a number of public and private institutions of higher education, and courts have frequently cited it as a basis for legal judgment. The statement was put out to "promote public understanding and support of academic freedom and tenure and agreement upon procedures to assure them in colleges and universities."[11] Its opening paragraph clearly refutes a concept of academic freedom as the property of a select handful: "Institutions of higher education are conducted for the common good and not to further the interest of either the individual teacher or the institution as a whole." Simultaneously, the statement warns the recipients of academic freedom against loose or provocative speech. A teacher, it urges, "should be careful not to introduce into his teaching controversial matter which has no relation to the subject" (p. 36).

The 1915 declaration also articulated four other enduring elements of academic freedom. The first was the now-familiar link between academic freedom and tenure, a job security meant to guard academic freedom itself. The second was a commitment to due process, a method of regulating academic life and employment. The third was peer review, the belief that one's colleagues and peers were the best judges of one's merit. Each of these concerned the professoriate. The fourth did not. Instead, taking up the rights of students, it asserted that freedom of learning was inseparable from freedom of teaching.

For some, the battle for academic freedom seems to have subsided, its last major campaigns waged during the McCarthy period of the 1950s. For others, of varying ideological persuasions, the Vietnam era may have been the last testing period of academic freedom. I believe, however, that this is far too sanguine, blind, and even self-deceiving a view in the 1980s, for academic freedom, if more established than it may have been in 1915 or 1940, is still comparatively fragile. Moreover, given the realities of the 1980s, we need to redefine and to broaden what it means to believe in academic freedom, and to work on its behalf. Let me outline three reasons for these conclusions.

First, despite such efforts as the 1940 statement, United States public opinion remains wary of academic freedom. In their massive study of attitudes towards civil liberties, Alida Brill and Herbert McClosky have found, for example, that only 41 percent of the public would permit college students to choose their own guest speakers. The public is even less willing to grant academic freedom to high school teachers than to professors. Only 25 percent would give such a teacher the right to express an opinion in class if that opinion went against a community's values or beliefs. The strongest support for academic freedom arises not from citizens at large but from "community leaders" and the "legal elite."[12]

One of the saddest, most unpalatable, truths about academic freedom is the fact that academic citizens themselves have often failed to rally to its defense. As people in general have passively watched violations of the Bill of Rights, so have we been guilty of complicity in violations of academic freedom. Many of us have not spoken up in its defense. We have feared loss of tenure, promotion, time, and colleagiality. The 1983 report of the MLA Task Force on Academic Freedom stated, tartly: "Whatever our motives, we have been, too often, cowardly lions in our own Oz."

Second, in the natural and (to a lesser degree) social sciences, restrictions on the free flow of information are becoming tighter and tighter. In a parallel development, the federal government is imposing strict censorship requirements on its employees. Indeed, more than 120,000 employees now working for the federal government have said, in writing, that they will submit for clearance any speech, article, or book they generate that concerns intelligence gathering. The survey that produced this figure excluded the CIA and the NSA. National security, the nature of corporate and proprietary research, and economic competition are some of the justifications for such restrictions. In October 1983, the American Association for the Advancement of Science felt compelled to organize a "Project on Secrecy and Openness in Scientific and Technical Communication."[13] Although humanists may think themselves exempt from such debates and struggles, academic freedom cannot be compartmentalized or departmentalized. What happens in the natural sciences will seep into the practice of the humanities.

Connections between various academic departments, however, are only part of a larger set of relations that matter if academic freedom is to flourish in the 1980s. According to the MLA Task Force report, academic freedom "can no more be separated from all people in education, or from education in general, than blood can be separated from the body in which it circulates." In other words, "any academic policy that tames the restlessness of intellect or impedes the open exchange of knowledge—no matter by whom it is initiated or on whom it falls—is a threat to academic freedom."[14]

Believers in academic freedom in United States higher education must reach out, then, to at least two other groups. The first consists of foreign scholars, whom United States academics have often supported. This group now includes scholars imprisoned in their own countries for their beliefs; foreign scholars and writers, like Carlos Fuentes and Gabriel García Márquez, who have had trouble entering the United States because of their politics; and scholars, like the late Angel Rama, whom immigration authorities suspect. The second group, local schools and libraries, has traditionally been less involved with United States higher education. From the perspective of academic freedom, the trouble that has received the most recent attention is censorship—in school and public libraries as well as in classrooms. Censorship has gnawed at books already written and textbooks in the process of being published or revised.[15] The philosophical and practical difficulties of selecting school and library materials are immense. At the elementary school level, where we can accurately refer to "the student" as "the child," and where the local tax-paying community supporting the school believes that the school, in turn, should support community and family values, perhaps we can hardly expect teachers to be given the latitude properly accorded to university faculties. In addition, faculty members may be condescending and insensitive when they hear censorious judgments about texts—for example, a wish to expel D. H. Lawrence's story "The Rocking Horse Winner" from a high school curriculum because it "has a touch of the occult, the bizarre, and ends in tragedy."[16]

Reacting only to the flat didacticism of such a statement, an English professor may miss its sincerity. Despite such reservations, I find it increasingly hard to limit academic freedom to higher education. Surely we can distinguish vigorously between an appropriate acquaintance with a family and community value system, on the one hand, and, on the other, a rigid indoctrination of students into the currently received wisdom of the local majority about culture. At some point, the teacher or librarian who acts *in loco parentis* as the expositor and repository of traditional values can become a distorter through oversimplification and withholding of alternative opinion. A past president of the AAUP has said: "Making the case for academic freedom in the public schools, and making teachers capable of using it, is the challenge of the next decade. It is much more difficult to do than most educators realize. Unquestionably, it is also of crucial importance to the future of genuine education in America."[17] Although my references to public opinion before revealed a suspicion of academic freedom, evidence also points to the possibility of flexibility on the issue. Forty-four percent of the people polled were "undecided" about whether high school teachers had the right to express an opinion in class if it went against a community's values and beliefs. Moreover, only 53 percent of the people polled, a bare majority, said that if a community paid a high school teacher's salary, that community had the right to keep its employee from teaching ideas that went against community standards.

My third reason for believing that academic freedom is neither stable nor serene arises from the present financial stringencies in higher education. In a number of blatant and subtle ways they constrict academic freedom, and redefining academic freedom today entails being aware of the consequences of institutional retrenchment. There are disquieting signs that the humanities—because they are experiencing declining enrollments in many places and because they do not generate a large base of external support—may be unusually vulnerable to financial pressures in the years immediately ahead.

To be sure, no logical connection exists between affluence and academic freedom. Wealthy institutions can be oppressive; impoverished ones more open. Nevertheless, such developments as "rollbacks" and "shrinkage" do threaten academic freedom. How? Such developments obviously increase instability in academic employment. They introduce new fears and concerns about getting and keeping a job, concerns that can lead to faculty self-censorship, especially in the advocacy of new ideas. Particularly endangered are innovative, fledgling programs in the humanities. Maintaining the status quo, as the "safer" course of action, deadens academic vitality and quality.

Unfortunately, too many of us have ridiculed, ignored, or misunderstood new scholarly subjects and methods—whether they concern women and gender, minority and ethnic groups, gays and lesbians, composition, or critical theory. In so doing, we have created a situation that itself hurts academic freedom, for we have done nothing less than undercut the self-proclaimed capacities for disinterestedness, impartiality, recognition of intellectual merit, and respect for the free play of ideas that we have traditionally used to justify academic freedom.

Another way in which present financial stringencies constrict academic freedom is that faculty members are also reluctant to criticize institutional policies and governance openly. To be sure, not all administrators use the harsh realities of budgets as a pious excuse to excise the holders of unpopular or unconventional opinions, to combine related departments after only token consultation with the affected faculty, or to eliminate departments with sturdy traditions but fragile enrollments. Some administrators do, however, and faculty may acquiesce.

Still another, and painful, way in which institutional retrenchment presses on academic freedom is in the treatment of nontenured faculty. They are now frequently subject to different evaluative standards from those of the past. Moreover, when cutbacks become mandatory, the last to be hired (very frequently women and minority faculty) are the first to go, a condition that parallels the threat to experimental programs. Workloads have increased in many places to the point where research is often impossible. In departments with large numbers of sections of required courses, almost always departments of English but often departments of foreign languages as well, faculties are flooded with part-timers. Lacking security and support, they are generally regarded and treated as second-class citizens by administrators and faculty alike. A generation of "gypsy scholars" has come into being, most of them the potential educators of the 1980s and 1990s. Accorded few rights, they function as the migrant workers of the academic industry. A bitterly ironic outcome of retrenchment has been the exclusion of many qualified academics from the arena in which they might have exercised their academic freedom. For them, academic freedom is no longer relevant.

Academic freedom, then, is at once an often-betrayed ideal; a legal, ethical, and institutional construct; and the underpinning of a process that mediates claims and beliefs about reality. It provides a field in which rows of ideas can grow. In theory, it contains all these ideas and endorses none of them. So construed, the idea of academic freedom now commands the allegiance of the broad center, the massive middle, of American higher education. It provides continuity and stability as other ideas, if they are in conflict, compete for attention and struggle for intellectual and curricular control of the middle.

Today, the intellectual and curricular middle is in flux, responding to contradictory forces. Pressing from the New Right is a theological fundamentalism with rigid theories of cultural authority. It is not afraid of trying to use organized politics (AIM, for example) to impose its cultural will. If the New Right manages to succeed, the middle will be far less secular and ecumenical than it now is. Pressing from another direction, from the Left, to point crudely, is a far more sophisticated, post-liberal set of interrogations. They are acutely attuned to the connections among culture and politics, and among the identities of powerful researchers and their findings, that dominant structures and ideologies produce.[18] More at home in "ordinary" colleges and universities than the theological fundamentalists, these interrogators are more influential in academic than "real world" politics. Their intellectual agenda, which I support, includes studies of differences (among women, between women and men, among classes and races); of everyday life; of the construction of sexualities and subjectivities; of the manufacture and reproduction of ideology and historical memory; of the placing of literature within cultural studies; and of the expansion of what "English" might mean and of what speaking, reading, and writing in English might be. If the Right is denunciatory and nostalgic, the Left is denunciatory and visionary.[19] Analytically, if the Left "succeeds," the middle will be far more taken up with the social constructon of meaning, interpretative methods, and cultural hierarchies and differences.

The struggle for the middle plays itself out in both vivid and muted ways. One of the more intense has been the selection of officials of federal cultural and educational agencies: the chair of the National Endowment for the Humanities; members of the NEH Council; the Archivist of the United States. A second has been the publication of dramatic, often overwrought, accounts of the failures of American education, educators, and dumbo students, all of whom regard "real" learning as if it were a white elephant. In 1987, two essays appeared that are calmer in tone, more civil in address than most recent commentary on education.[20] The more highly publicized is the more conservative: "American Memory," by Lynne V. Cheney. In her essay, Cheney maintains that education must transmit culture, particularly the *great* books of literature and *great* events of history. The antithesis of greatness is the trendy. Transmission asks students to *master* content, a body of knowledge. Textbooks, in today's classrooms, pervert culture and hobble mastery. Relying on the language of a comfortable humanism, Cheney insists that the past, taught well, will help us realize our "human potential," "affirm our humanity," and assist us in finding its "essence" (6–7). Such realizations, affirmations, and assistance have a political purpose, for historical consciousness builds community. It is a "civic glue." Moreover, a proper education will stall the decline in America's global position by offering better workers and the ability to export ideas that are at once "the best" and democratic. Carefully, Cheney balances her calls for excellence with a prudent recognition of the need for "educational equity"; her calls for the teaching of history with a recognition of the history of women and minorities; her calls for a national renewal, through a revivified national memory that touches "the better angels of our nature," with a recognition of the interdependence of the globe's nations. Her reforms, however, speak more passionately of restoration and rejuvenation than of recreation.

The lesser known and more magisterially historical essay is "The Humanities and the American Promise," written by Merrill D. Peterson as the "report" of the Colloquium on the Humanities and the American People. Significantly, if Cheney's title evokes "memory," the past, Peterson's evokes "promise," the future. No postmodernist, Peterson nevertheless says that the humanities "represent the *striving* for coherence and synthesis" (3, my italics). Supportive of both reflection and critical thought, the humanities "may be and often are disturbers of the peace" (5). Like Cheney, Peterson believes that the health of the humanities and of the polity are inseparable. However, his America has never had a common culture. Indeed, constructing a "common cultural vocabulary" is perilous. What Americans share is an often-debased set of political principles that value "freedom, equality, and self-government" (5). They stimulate a culture that prizes openness and diversity. Peterson supports the new scholarship about women, ethnicity, and people of color that reflects and codifies those virtues; for him, the most marvelous of American poets is Walt Whitman, who sang of them. If academicians are to be genuine humanists, they will act in the spirit of Whitman. They will defy disciplinary rigidities, invidious distinctions between academic and non-academic humanists, and the ties and binds of wearing traditions. The middle will celebrate itself and others.

Deliberately, I have deployed a vocabulary of struggle and conflict. In heavy measure, politics is a domain in which people engage in, avoid, or are forbidden a struggle and conflict about the dispensation of power, justice, and resources. I have attempted to outline some of the politics of research in the contemporary humanities. I hope that I have not lined out. Our ideas about gender, people of color, and language are crucial sites of a struggle and conflict that is not yet resolved. Indeed, some of the actors at these sites believe resolution theoretically or practically impossible. In the West, a canonical work about conflict, which all proponents of national security ought to read, is *The Peloponnesian War.* In book 7, Thucydides is telling the story of the Sicilian campaign that will end in disaster for the Athenians who have so ignorantly, so stupidly embarked upon a war of conquest. Trying to take a camp at Epipolae, the Athenians find themselves in a confusing battle at night. Thucydides comments: "[I]t was not easy to get from one side or the other any detailed account of the affair. . . . [I]n a night engagement . . . how could anyone know anything for certain? Although there was a bright moon they saw each other only as men do by moonlight, that is to say, they could distinguish the form of the body, but could not tell for certain whether it was a friend or an enemy. . . . Owing to the rout that had taken place all in front was now in confusion, and the noise made it difficult to distinguish anything."[21] Thucydides reminds us of two confusions, two shadows of doubt, that feed on each other: the confusion of the participants in history as they breathe, run, fight, and die; and the confusion of the historian who must wire a memory bank. Anyone engaged in research, and inevitably in the politics of research, must remember his warnings. However, they need not be-

smirch the promise of a new politics of research that seeks to ally consciousness and a genuine cultural democracy. Greatness and brightness will
fall from the air, from us, perhaps from almost everywhere.

Notes

1 *AIM Report* (October-B 1986); 1–4. Dues and contributions to AIM are tax-
deductible.
2 See Peter D. Dresser, ed., *Research Centers Directory,* 12th edition, 2 vols. (De-
troit: Gale Research Co., 1988).
3 Karen J. Winkler, "Researchers in American Studies Shortchange Ethnic and Minority Groups, Scholars Charge," *Chronicle of Higher Education* (December 9,
1987), A–4, 5, 6.
4 Introduction to *Research Centers Directory,* pp. 7–8. *Humanities Programs 1987*
(New York: Foundation Center, 1987) reports that 74 foundations made 138 grants,
totaling $20,149,387, in the humanities to universities, colleges, schools, and as-
sociations. I picked up three major patterns of funding: a) a little to state councils
for the humanities; b) a great deal to established, mainstream institutions such as
the Aspen Institute, Newberry Library, American Council for Learned Societies,
National Humanities Center; c) some for teaching outside of liberal arts settings,
for example, in high schools, medical and other professional schools.
5 *Arts and Cultural Programs* (New York: Foundation Center, 1987). Karen Roth-
myer, "Citizen Scaife," in *Speak Out Against the New Right,* edited by Herbert F.
Vetter (Boston: Beacon Press, 1982), pp. 22–36, outlines the career of Richard
Scaife, who controls the Sarah Scaife Foundation and a cluster of related organizations.
6 *Grants for Women and Girls* (New York: Foundation Center, 1987), p. 105.
7 New York: St. Martin's Press, 1987.
8 Washington, D.C.: National Endowment for the Humanities, 1987, p. 7.
9 The Foundation Center in New York issues quarterly profiles, *Source Book Profile,*
of the one thousand largest foundations in the United States, invaluable sources of
information about income, goals, funded projects, and administration.
10 *Academic Freedom and Tenure: A Handbook of the AAUP,* edited by Louis Joughin
(Madison: University of Wisconsin Press, 1969), p. 158. My service as chair of the
Task Force on Academic Freedom of the Modern Language Association, and then
as chair of the Committee on Academic Freedom of the MLA, has influenced the
following pages. They are also deeply indebted to the Task Force's "Report of the
Task Force on Academic Freedom," Modern Language Association, May 1983,
and to my colleagues on that task force. Michael Ryan, *Marxism and Deconstruction: A Critical Articulation* (Baltimore: Johns Hopkins Press, 1982), pp. 132–58,
strongly argues for "an alternative principle" of academic freedom.
11 Joughin, ed., *Academic Freedom and Tenure,* p. 34.
12 Herbert McClosky and Alida Brill, *Dimensions of Tolerance: What Americans*

Believe About Civil Liberties (New York: Russell Sage Foundation, 1983), pp. 54–58.

13 See American Association for the Advancement of Science press release on "Project on Secrecy and Openness," 1515 Massachusetts Avenue N.W., Washington, D.C. 20005, October 1983, p. 3.

14 Walter B. Metzger, "Symposium on Academic Freedom," *New York University Education Quarterly* 13, no. 3 (Spring 1982): 5. In the same symposium, William Van Alstyne offers a narrower, but informed, concept of academic freedom.

15 According to a 1982 survey by the Committee Against Censorship of the National Council of Teachers of English and the Wisconsin Council of Teachers of English, the most censored books in high school libraries are Anonymous, *Go Ask Alice;* J. D. Salinger, *Catcher in the Rye;* Boston Women's Health Collective, *Our Bodies, Ourselves;* Judy Blume, *Forever;* John Steinbeck, *Of Mice and Men;* Alice Childress, *A Hero Ain't Nothing But a Sandwich;* Paul Zindel, *My Darling, My Hamburger;* Kurt Vonnegut, *Slaughterhouse Five;* John Steinbeck, *The Grapes of Wrath;* Mark Twain, *Huckleberry Finn.*

16 "Minority Report to the (Alabama) State Board of Education Concerning Textbook Adoption," (Alabama) State Textbook Commission, December 7, 1982, p. 3.

17 William Van Alstyne, "Symposium on Academic Freedom," p. 4.

18 A recent array of such ideas is Cary Nelson and Lawrence Grossberg, eds., *Marxism and the Interpretation of Culture* (Urbana and Chicago: University of Illinois Press, 1988). The book began as a series of events, including an international conference at the University of Illinois in 1983. The events were financed by twelve centers and programs at the University, nine departments, and the National Endowment for the Humanities. This shows how radical projects must hunt for funds and, yet, how the funds can be there, in dribs and drabs.

19 In *Nostalgia and Sexual Difference,* Janice Doane and Devon Hodges acutely dissect a New Right and neoconservative scenario about the past that embraces patriarchal authority and referential certainties (New York: Methuen, Inc., 1987, p. 160).

20 Lynne V. Cheney, "American Memory: A Report on the Humanities in the Nation's Public Schools" (Washington, D.C.: National Endowment for the Humanities, 1987), and Merrill D. Peterson (on behalf of the Colloquium on the Humanities and the American People), "The Humanities and the American Promise" (October 1987). The Division of State Programs of NEH funded the colloquium, but a 1986 grant of the Joyce Foundation made publication possible and the Texas Committee for the Humanities made distribution possible.

21 Thucydides, *The Complete Writings,* introduced by John H. Finley, Jr. (New York: Modern Library, 1951), pp. 425–56.

Teach the Conflicts

An Alternative to Educational Fundamentalism

Gerald Graff

In grappling with any problem, it makes sense to start by asking whether we have defined it in a productive way. We naturally want to set tasks that lend themselves to solutions and not waste time complaining about things we have little chance of changing for the better. Yet it seems that when we minister to educational institutions, we habitually formulate their problems in ways that not only are unproductive but also virtually guarantee defeat. We put the blame on causes which we are unlikely to be able to change, and which may not even warrant changing.

I am thinking of the habit of blaming the problems of higher education on the loss of a collectively shared purpose, vision, or mission. Over and over today we hear that the university has lost its sense of purpose, that the college curriculum is drifting without a coherent direction, that it no longer stands for any substantive intellectual goal. Above all, it is said that the curriculum has been trivialized by the abandonment of its traditional emphasis on content.

This diagnosis received wide public circulation in 1984, when National Endowment for the Humanities chairman William Bennett (soon to be named Secretary of Education) published his study group report, "To Reclaim a Legacy." Students, said the report, come to the university expecting that "its leaders have a clear vision of what is worth knowing and what is important in our heritage that all educated persons should know."[1] What they usually find is that "many of our colleges and universities have lost a clear sense of the importance of the humanities and the purpose of education" (16).

The tremors had hardly died down from Bennett's remarks when two surprisingly best-selling books set them off again. In *The Closing of the American Mind,* Allan Bloom stated that in the university today, "there is no vision, nor is there a set of competing visions, of what an educated human being is."[2] In *Cultural Literacy,* E. D. Hirsch, writing of the lower schools, asserted that "during recent decades Americans have hesitated to make a decision about the specific knowledge that children need to learn in school."[3] Secretary Bennett had put the blame on "a failure of nerve and faith" on the part of educators. Hirsch blamed the shift to teaching "skills" that results when educators feel they are unable to agree on a common content. Bloom blamed philosophical relativism, seen especially in the fetish of remaining "open" to every point of view, however foolish.

In case anyone had still not got the message, it was further underscored by another book, published around the same time as those of Bloom and Hirsch. In *College: The Undergraduate Experience in America,* Ernest L. Boyer, president of the Carnegie Foundation on the Advancement of Teaching, declared that undergraduate colleges had undergone a loss of "their sense of mission" and a "confusion over goals." The colleges, said Boyer, are "confused about their mission and how to impart shared values on which the vitality of both higher education and society depends."[4] The drift toward incoherence could only continue, Boyer feared, until we "gain greater clarity about the mission of the college" (262). To gain this clarity we would have to ask such fundamental questions as, "What is most worth knowing? What is it that colleges believe students need to know and understand as well as be able to do?" (32).

I give the name "educational fundamentalism" to this tendency to blame the crisis of higher education and the humanities on a loss of consensus about fundamental purposes. Educational fundamentalism is usually thoroughly secular (in fact, for religious fundamentalists it is often too secular—as in their reaction against the secular humanism of Secretary Bennett), but it is "fundamentalist" in its belief in the primacy of fundamental truths and values. Schematically stated, the fundamentalist analysis runs as follows:

1. The college curriculum has come to be determined by market-demand and interest-group politics rather than by a coherent educational rationale.

2. Unable to agree on a common content for education, educators pass the buck to the students in a "cafeteria-counter" (alternatively, "Chinese menu," "department store," "garage sale") of options, desperately hoping that students will somehow make sense of what the educators themselves have given up hoping to control.

3. As consensus wanes on educational ends, instrumental means take the place of ends or become ends in themselves. For students, the content of college experience becomes a mechanical accumulation of course credits; for professors, a mechanical accumulation of research, which is piled up at the expense of higher responsibilities to undergraduate teaching.

4. The solution is for universities to go back to requiring a more or less fixed canon of great books (Bennett, Bloom), while schools supply the cultural literacy which will enable students to read these and other books (Hirsch). The cure is an "integrated core" of general education courses, which will synthesize the latent areas of universal common ground across departments (Boyer).

These proposals differ in matters of detail and political coloration. Hirsch, for example, justifies cultural literacy in populist terms and disclaims any necessary link with Bennett's or Bloom's traditional canon. But different as the proposals may be, the message heard by the public tends to be the same. It speaks persuasively to a citizenry weary of decades of ideological quarreling, impatient with professorial equivocations, and eager for simple, no-nonsense answers and practical action. What could be more practical, in a situation where we have lost touch with a common content in education, than to go back to basic content–questions like the ones put by Boyer: "What is most worth knowing? What is it that colleges believe students need to know and understand as well as be able to do?"

There is no point denying that educational fundamentalism has struck a nerve, and its diagnosis cannot be dismissed as wholly wrong. What makes the fundamentalist analysis persuasive is the manifest fact that American higher education is indeed confused and does lack a sense of common purpose. Educational fundamentalists are right about the incoherence of the curriculum, and they are also right in tracing this incoherence to the fact that the curriculum is determined not by an integrated educational philosophy but by a political "let's make a deal" game of competing interest groups. The curriculum has indeed been rendered incoherent by the fact that we respond to disagreement by separating into individual compartments regulated by the rule of laissez-faire. Detecting a coherent pattern in even a single academic discipline under such an uncoordinated system must be rather like trying to understand the game of baseball by watching individual pitchers, batters, fielders, and umpires all working out separately.

What remains doubtful, however, is whether injecting a common purpose into higher education is a realistic or desirable alternative to organized laissez-faire. The fundamentalists are right to locate the educational problem in the incoherence and disconnection of the university's parts. Where they go wrong is in thinking that the only way to counteract incoherence and disconnection is to legislate a common content—a synthesizable group of principles, concepts, texts, or vocabularies of literacy which will integrate the dispersed parts. Their mistake is to confuse coherence with consensus.

The fundamentalists never ask themselves what is to be done when educators *do* revive questions like "what is most worth knowing?" and "what is our image of an educated person?"—only to discover, as they have so often discovered in the past, that there is no agreement on these questions, either among themselves or in the culture at large. Hirsch begins to raise the issue, but only to evade it, when he states that the question of who is to define the content of American education "must not be allowed to serve its traditional role as a debate-stopper" (144). Indeed it should not serve that role, but Hirsch does not address the problem of what is to be done when the debate over content continues but reaches no resolution. In such a situation, there is a certain futility in complaining over and over that we must recover a consensus on educational content. Whose content? Consensus on whose terms? As for the charges of relativism, they point to a genuine philosophical and cultural problem. But much of what is currently attacked as relativism is only the recognition that, for most important subjects, conflicting approaches are possible.

The fundamentalist educational program legitimates itself by constructing a myth of history, which maintains that cultural and educational consensus was intact until very recently and therefore is recoverable now. Bennett, for example, speaks as if restoring consensus is a simple matter of discarding the aberrant permissiveness of the 1960s (when educators presumably lost their nerve), which temporarily jogged American education off its accustomed track. There has in fact been a greater degree of consensus on the content of education in the past, but this consensus has been eroding seriously since the end of the nineteenth century, when American education began to be transformed from an institution mainly devoted to the transmission of Christian orthodoxy into a democratic institution promoting free intellectual inquiry. In my recent history of literary studies in America, *Professing Literature,* I show that today's laments of lost consensus unwittingly repeat a refrain that was already a commonplace a century ago.[5] When the university did enjoy a relative consensus on ends and values, this was only because it excluded or subordinated major segments of the population (Jews, nonwhites, women, and others). It is as these groups have entered or gained more power in the university that consensus has broken down.

The current attempts to equip higher education with an integrated content are only the latest in a long series of such efforts, which have always ended in educational futility. There is virtually nothing in the Bennett-Bloom-Hirsch-Boyer program which was not already spelled out in the model of general education first developed at Columbia University after World War I and extended in the 1930s at the University of Chicago in the Great Books program of Robert Maynard Hutchins and Mortimer J. Adler, and again at Harvard after World War II in the so-called Harvard Redbook, *General Education in a Free Society.* Adler, in fact, was recently quoted (in *Time*) as saying that "everything [Allan] Bloom complains about" in *The Closing of the American Mind* "is what . . . Robert Hutchins and I talked about in the '30's."[6]

The failure of all these attempts at integration was inevitable, because in a complex modern university any proposed principle of integration will be either too narrowly defined to secure agreement or too broadly defined to be meaningful. If the principle is given enough definition to carry bite, the faculty and students rebel against it, as they did against the Hutchins-Adler plan at Chicago. If the principle is diluted in order to gain faculty and student support, its content becomes so bland as to be meaningless—the fate of the Harvard Redbook.

But these attempts at educational unification do not simply fail. They invariably provoke a counterreaction which ushers in an even more extreme state of fragmentation than the previous one. Then, too, the break in continuity that results from the alternation of rebellion and backlash tends to erase the memory of previous failures. No doubt this explains why those who advocate restoring the values of the past rarely seem to learn anything from the past.

Paradoxically, the idea that a consensus on objectives is a prerequisite of institutional action tends to undermine belief in the very possibility of collective effort. Once the hope of agreeing on educational content is disappointed, that content is left to be determined by individual instructors in the uncoordinated way the educational critics deplore. When this disappointment has been repeated, departments lose faith in the very possibility of acting collectively. The result is a contraction of vision, in which the initial project of reshaping the institution as a whole is reduced to piecemeal efforts—always too little and too late—at improving individual teaching practices. Once it is assumed that collective action would require consensus and that such consensus is unachievable, then the single, autonomous course becomes the largest unit over which anyone can imagine exercising control. In such a situation there appears to be no point in asking how students may be experiencing the curricular aggregate, because there appears to be nothing anyone can do about it.

In the academic humanities, it is obvious that ideological divisions have become so severe as to make the chances of a consensus in the foreseeable future very unlikely. It is symptomatic that the very words *humanities, humanistic,* and *human* are honorific terms in one current literary-critical vocabulary and terms of abuse in another. Conflicts have arisen over the very meaning of terms like *literature* and *criticism.* Concepts that were once taken for granted (such as text, culture, interpretation, author, reader, reading, self, value, and historical period), as well as the terms and methods in which these concepts are argued, have become openly controversial. Disputes over the jargon used by literary theorists and other avant-garde critics generate so much heat because they are really philosophical and political disputes over larger stakes. It is not a purely literary question whether literature is taught "for its own sake" or the sake of universal humanistic truths, or for the way it "inscribes" conflicts of class, nationality, race, and gender.

Among the issues at stake in such disputes is the consequence of assigning autonomous departmental status to the category of literature, bureaucratically separating it from philosophy, history, psychology, social thought, media studies, and the sciences. For many older scholars, territorial demarcations like "literature" (or "English," "French," etc.) are merely neutral bureaucratic pigeonholes which enable literary study to get on efficiently with its proper business. From this viewpoint, there is no reason to fuss over such demarcations, especially since they less and less delimit the actual interests of those who work within them.

For the critical Left, on the other hand, such departmental boundaries are not neutral methodological divisions, but things which have an ideological effect by predefining and restricting the kinds of questions thought to be legitimate within each field. Keeping "English," for example, departmentally separate from history and social theory helps prevent students from asking ideological questions about literature and criticism, since these questions tend to appear extrinsic to the field. The often confused debate over whether or not texts can have determinate meanings is, at its most interesting, a political debate over whether the contexts of reading should be officially regulated and delimited. The theory that meaning is indeterminate is often really an assertion of the right to read texts in contexts other than those officially sanctioned by the institution.

The pervasiveness of this and other forms of explicit "politicization" of literary studies causes the blood of many traditional humanists to boil, for they are not persuaded that the questions raised by theorists about the political consequences of culture are proper ones. These humanists have every right to pursue their own questions in their own way, but the issue is whether they should have the right to keep the theorists' questions from occupying the forefront of the discipline with their own. The issue has been all but decided (though not in every institution or department), for the new and heretofore unsanctioned questions about the politics of literature and criticism have achieved increasing legitimacy, whether or not one accepts the theorists' answers to them. It seems obvious that these political questions will not be made to disappear by ritualistic denunciations of politicization, relativism, and failures of nerve.

Here, then, is my proposal. In the face of this political challenge, it would be wise for humanities departments to confront it and try to exploit whatever is educationally productive in it rather than sit around hoping that it will go away. This would also be a more practical strategy, for a consensus is not likely to be arrived at soon, and the standard alternative to consensus—armed truce based on mutual agreement not to confront disagreements, lest the students find out about them—only deepens the fragmentation and curricular log-rolling that traditionalists themselves deplore.

In other words, in a situation where consensus is hard to come by, there are practical advantages to abandoning the search for it and looking for ways to make the disagreements over ends, values, and methods into a principle of educational coherence. It is possible to imagine models of coherence that would not require everyone to agree on some single definition of what is worth knowing or teaching. If the ideological conflicts in the humanities are unlikely to eventuate in a common content for education, why not try to make these conflicts themselves the basis for a more coherent study of culture? Why not look at ideological and methodological disagreement as a potential opportunity instead of a paralyzing condition to be cured? If the curriculum must be a political game of "let's make a deal" (and arguably that is always what it has been), then we might at least place in the foreground whatever larger questions of principle are at stake in the game.

An obvious objection will be that, if faculties have been unable to agree on first principles, there is little reason to think they will be able to disagree about those principles in productive ways. The same factors that have blocked any effort at consensus will also block the effort to agree to disagree. It is difficult to stage a dispute when the parties cannot even agree on the vocabulary in which disputes are to be conducted. Moving from a consensus-model to a conflict-model (the objection runs) would only intensify current confusion and incoherence while doing away with what is left of academic civility. It would also further confuse students, already sufficiently confused by the surrounding dissonance.

There is certainly a danger in putting too much stress on *conflict*. If this word seems needlessly confrontational, it may be more useful to think of what I am proposing as a "conversational" or "dialogical" model, which would need to become conflictual only in certain contexts. Conflict presupposes consensus, because in order for conflict to arise there has to be agreement on what is important to fight over. I give priority to conflict because important institutional and cultural-political conflicts do exist, and (to invoke a Freudian axiom) when we avoid confronting them and working them through, these conflicts have a way of coming back to haunt us. The institutional history of the humanities (as narrated in *Professing Literature*) is a classic instance of this immobilizing repetition-syndrome.

I do not minimize the difficulties of staging conflicts coherently in a scene notoriously rife with noncommunicating discourses. We should be careful, however, not to confuse staging conflict with disputation or with getting colleagues "talking to one another," these being one—but only one—means to an end. There may be numerous ways of staging a conflict, not all of them requiring that opposing parties debate one another face-to-face. The important thing is not that professional factions talk to one another (though this may help in many cases), but that a way be found to help students see what is at stake in the professional and cultural conflicts that surround them.

Why it has been difficult for students to see these conflicts has to do with the way the field-structure of the university effaces both intellectual conflict and identity. Since it became professionalized in the 1870s and 1880s, the modern university has claimed to represent a unified body of knowledge, but it has assumed that this unified knowledge is most effectively pursued by encouraging widely diversified forms of inquiry. The departmental structure of the university has therefore been organized upon a principle of increasingly proliferating difference. It is animated by the idea of representing various kinds of difference—in subjects, ideologies, intellectual approaches, methodologies, values, and conceptions of culture. Yet the university organizes itself in a way that effaces or muffles the very differences it encourages. The university embodies central conflicts of both the larger culture and the narrower professional culture, but its structure prevents these conflicts from becoming visible *as* conflicts. And when conflicts are not visible as conflicts, identities and similarities become equally invisible.

The problem is that neither difference nor identity can become functional for students and other outsiders unless the two are experienced *as* difference or identity. And neither difference nor identity can be experienced as such when disparate interests, approaches, and ideologies are encountered only in separation from one another. The working axiom here is that it is difficult for us to identify the aims of any social institution if we rarely see its members functioning together. To the degree that any institution masks the relations among its members, it tends to make itself functionally invisible to outsiders. This result is especially damaging in education insofar as learning is inherently dialogical, relational, and differential. Objects of study become mysterious when prevented from being seen in their difference from other objects.

There is a real risk that altering the pattern I have just described would only deepen student confusions. But staying with the pattern has its risks too. We need to ask whether confusion has really been held at bay by the practice of protecting students from premature exposure to intellectual dissonance. There is something curious about the standard academic assumption that only in the advanced stages of disciplinary inquiry do students qualify to be let in on the news that the experts frequently disagree. The deeper sources of student confusion may lie not in the conflicts in and between the disciplines, but in the failure of the university to negotiate these conflicts out in the open where students would have a chance to grasp what is at stake. Allan Bloom is surely wrong when he says that in the university there is no "set of competing visions . . . of what an educated human being is" (337). But Bloom would be right if he said that the competition of those visions is not openly dramatized.

When we conceive a department or a curriculum as an entity that "covers" a series of autonomous fields, we leave no agency responsible for the contexts in which these fields are studied or for any questions about how the fields are related or why they are defined as they are. As long as faculty and students cover the requisite areas, questions about the ways in which various ideas and values studied within these areas may connect, coincide, or conflict need not arise. The field coverage model makes the department virtually self-regulating and self-administering: as long as all fields are staffed and covered by students, the net result—the transmission of humanistic values—supposedly takes care of itself, so that no debate need arise about it. As long as field coverage is the only model, it will be hard to conceive alternatives to the present structure.

Alternatives are also discouraged, however, by the ingrained assumption that the basic unit of education and pedagogy must always be the individual *course*. Like the coverage model, courses are eminently efficient to administer and they appeal to the individualistic ethos which is traditional to teaching. The department chair need only assign the appropriate courses to the faculty at the start of the year, and the rest will take care of itself. Convenient though this arrangement is, it exacts a great price, since courses are inherently privatizing: they block the development of an academic public sphere. While inside their courses, students and teachers are cut off from what is happening in other courses and largely prevented from finding out. No wonder academics are always complaining about lack of "community," when they spend so much of their time isolated from one another in courses.

In theory, every academic course is *about* other courses as well as its own concerns. In reality too this is often the case, for courses can hardly help intersecting in potentially interesting ways. But teachers and students are only rarely in a position to recognize these moments of intersection, much less to exploit them. Academic courses form an implicit conversation, but it is one that the courses themselves prevent from becoming internally responsive.

What is needed is a more collective model of teaching and learning, one that does not efface the relations and differences among subjects, theories, ideologies, contexts, and methods but brings them into the foreground. Some success has already been achieved by team-teaching and the clustering of courses around common themes. Taking the idea a bit further, one could imagine something that might be called a "metacourse," whose aim would be not to expound its own subject matter so much as to correlate and recontextualize issues raised in other courses. A current Northwestern University graduate student, John Lavelle, describes such a course he took as a Notre Dame undergraduate, team-taught by a sociologist, a literary critic, a philosopher, and a political scientist and open to students of all majors. Lavelle says that, as a result of the course, "I became more aware of the contexts and methods of my other courses, could fit certain professors into general categories and bring alternative perspectives to my studies." Most interestingly, Lavelle says the course helped him make sense even of disciplines that did not participate in it. "A strength of the course," he writes, "was its freedom to tolerate the intransigence of established departments by making them objects of discussion. Stubborn silence was one aspect of the conversation among others."

Another idea (which I explain more fully in an article in the *Yale Journal of Criticism*)[7] would be for groups of teachers, instead of "teaming," to exchange courses in mid-semester. Teacher A would ask Teacher B's students to reformulate B's points and assumptions and then (tactfully, to be sure) would raise challenging questions about them, while Teacher B meanwhile would do the same thing with the students of Teacher A. I know the kinds of anxieties such a format would arouse in some students and teachers, but it could have a significant effect even without full participation by faculty and students. The format would enable teachers to engage their different approaches and draw the class into the discussion, but they would not have to get prior agreement or even to be sure at the outset about their final positions.

A third tactic would supplement existing courses with something akin to an academic conference. Conferences have become increasingly popular among university faculty, because they offer forms of intellectual community that are missing from the everyday routine of teaching and research. One could imagine a literature department breaking for a week during the semester for a joint conference that would give focus to issues and contexts common to several courses. An outside visitor or two could be invited to stimulate the discussion. Students could be assigned to plan and run the conference, present papers and critiques, or write papers about it afterwards.

These innovations would inject an element of collective discussion and dispute into teaching and learning within a structure not radically different from the familiar one, so that confusion would not reign. They would tend to relativize the teacher's authority and the course content without doing away with them. By putting teachers in a position to make use of one another's ideas and expertise in a way they currently cannot, such innovations would help relieve the feeling teachers often have of needing in each class to reconstruct the whole inventory of civilization from scratch, out of their unaided resources. At worst, they should provide a more effective means of inculcating the cultural literacy Hirsch rightly calls for than Hirsch's unlearnable lists of disjointed factoids. Cultural literacy would then be treated not as a neutral body of "background information" to be processed but as something itself open to interrogation and dispute.

One does not have to reject the idea of the disciplines as a body of knowledge in order to see that, even in the hardest of hard sciences, the "body" is no longer an integrated whole that speaks with one consensual voice. In fact, as the intellectual disciplines have moved progressively away from the positivism of the nineteenth century, knowledge has tended to be conceived not as a unified structure so much as a conversation. Even a disorderly conversation, in which all parties speak at once and do not listen, is one from which participants and eavesdroppers can learn something, if only why some discourses have no basis for arguing with one another.

The educational fundamentalists' demand for an integrated educational content has always failed in the past, and it will fail again today, as it richly deserves to do. The point is not that the traditional questions about what is worth studying and teaching are no longer worth asking, but that these questions need to be restated in a way that acknowledges their controversial character as well as the institutional realities of how they typically get resolved or remain unresolved. It is not that content does not matter, but that what is meant by "content" needs to be rethought when we cannot count on agreement about what it should be.

Notes

Portions of this essay in a different version appeared under the title "Conflicts Over the Curriculum Are Here to Stay; They Should Be Made Educationally Productive," in *The Chronicle of Higher Education* (17 February 1988).

1 William Bennett, "To Reclaim a Legacy," *Chronicle of Higher Education* 29.14 (28 November 1984): 18.
2 Allan Bloom, *The Closing of the American Mind* (New York: Simon and Schuster, 1987), p. 337.
3 E. D. Hirsch, *Cultural Literacy: What Every American Needs to Know* (New York: Houghton Mifflin, 1987), p. 19.
4 Ernest Boyer, *College: The Undergraduate Experience in America,* Report of the Carnegie Foundation on the Advancement of Teaching (New York: Harper and Row, 1987), p. 3.
5 Gerald Graff, *Professing Literature: An Institutional History* (Chicago: University of Chicago Press, 1987); see especially chapters 6, 7, and 10.
6 Mortimer J. Adler, quoted in *Time,* 130.7 (17 August 1987): 57.
7 Graff, "What Should We Be Teaching—When There's No 'We'?" *Yale Journal of Criticism* 1. 2 (1987): 189–211.

Contributors

Betty Jean Craige, a professor of comparative literature at the University of Georgia, is author of *Lorca's Poet in New York: The Fall into Consciousness, Literary Relativity,* and *Reconnection: Dualism to Holism in Literary Study* (published by the University of Georgia Press); translator of *Selected Poems of Antonio Machado, The Poetry of Gabriel Celaya,* and *Manuel Mantero: New Songs for the Ruins of Spain;* and editor of *Relativism in the Arts* (also published by the University of Georgia Press). She has served on the board of the Georgia Endowment for the Humanities and on the MLA Commission on the Status of Women in the Profession.

Henry Louis Gates, Jr., currently a professor of English, comparative literature, and Africana studies at Cornell University, was a MacArthur Prize Fellow (1981–1986) and a winner of numerous other grants and awards. He has written *The Signifying Monkey: Towards a Theory of Afro-American Literary Criticism* and *Figures in Black: Words, Signs, and the Racial Self* and has edited many books, among them *"Race," Writing, and Difference, The Classic Slave Narrative, In the House of Osugbo: Critical Essays on Wole Soyinka, The Oxford-Schomburg Library of Nineteenth-Century Black Women's Writings,* and *Wole Soyinka: A Bibliography* (with J. Gibbs and K. Katrak). Dr. Gates has served on the editorial boards of *PMLA, Critical Inquiry, American Quarterly, Studies in American Fiction,* and *Black American Literature Forum.* He is general editor of *The Norton Anthology of Afro-American Literature.*

Gerald Graff, John C. Shaffer Professor of Humanities and English at Northwestern University, and former chair of the English department, is author of

Literature Against Itself: Literary Ideas in Modern Society, Poetic Statement and Critical Dogma, and *Professing Literature: An Institutional History.* He is the editor, with Reginald Gibbons, of *Criticism in the University* and, with Michael Warner, of a forthcoming historical anthology, *The Origins of Literary Studies in America.*

Annette Kolodny, dean of the Faculty of Humanities and a professor of English at the University of Arizona, won the Florence Howe Essay Prize for Feminist Criticism in 1979 for "Dancing Through the Minefield: Some Observations on the Theory, Practice, and Politics of a Feminist Literary Criticism." She is author of the books *The Land Before Her: Fantasy and Experience of the American Frontiers, 1630–1860* and *The Lay of the Land: Metaphor as Experience and History in American Life and Letters,* as well as numerous articles and chapters, including "The Integrity of Memory: Creating a New Literary History of the United States," "A Map for Re-Reading: Gender and the Interpretation of Literary Texts," and "Some Notes on Defining a 'Feminist Literary Criticism.' " She has served on the advisory or editorial boards of *American Literature, Early American Literature, Genders: An Interdisciplinary Journal,* and *Arizona Quarterly.*

Paul Lauter, recently appointed the Allen K. and Gwendolyn Miles Smith Professor of English at Trinity College in Hartford, Connecticut, has written two books with Florence Howe, *The Conspiracy of the Young* and *The Impact of Women's Studies on the Campus and the Disciplines,* and has edited *Theories of Comedy, The Politics of Literature* (with Louis Kampf), and *Reconstructing American Literature: Courses, Syllabi, Issues.* He is coordinating editor for *A Reconstructed Anthology of American Literature,* to be published by D. C. Heath in 1989, and he is working on two other books on the American literary canon. He has served on the editorial boards of *Radical Teacher* and *Signs: A Journal of Women in Culture and Society.*

Ellen Messer-Davidow, an assistant professor of English at the University of Minnesota, has edited with Joan Hartman the volumes *Women in Print I* and *Women in Print II,* published by the MLA. She is the author of "The Philosophical Bases of Feminist Literary Criticisms," which appeared in *New Literary History* (Fall 1987). She has also published articles in *The Road Retaken: Women Re-enter the Academy,* edited by Irene Thompson and Audrey Roberts, and in *Signs* and *Journal of Thought.* She is now editing with Antony H. Harrison a book titled *Rewriting English Literary History from Feminist Perspectives* and with Joan Hartman a book titled *Critical Issues in Feminist Inquiry.*

Catharine R. Stimpson, a professor of English and dean of the Graduate School at Rutgers University, was the founding editor of *Signs: Journal of Women in Culture and Society* and is now the editor of a book series for the University of Chicago Press. She was the first director of the Women's Center of Barnard College and of the Institute for Research on Women at Rutgers, and she has served as chair of the New York State Council for the Humanities, of the *Ms. Magazine* Board of Scholars, and of the National Council for Research on Women. Dr. Stimpson has written *J. R. R. Tolkien, Class Notes* (a novel), and over eighty monographs, short stories, essays, and reviews in such journals as *Aphra, Transatlantic Review, Nation, New York Times Book Review, Critical Inquiry, Boundary 2*, and *Woman in Sexist Society*. She has edited *Women and National Development* and coedited *Women—Sex and Sexuality*. Recently elected second vice-president, Stimpson will serve as president of the Modern Language Association in 1990.

Ana Celia Zentella is an associate professor of black and Puerto-Rican studies at Hunter College and is in the linguistics doctoral program at the CUNY Graduate Center. She is a sociolinguist whose University of Pennsylvania dissertation of Spanish-English code-switching was awarded first place in the Outstanding Dissertation Competition sponsored by the National Advisory Council on Bilingual Education, and she has published numerous articles on Latino language and culture in the United States. She is currently a board member of the New York Council for the Humanities and of the Educational Fund of the National Congress for Puerto Rican Rights.